MW01644300

EA[illegible] BOOK SERIES REVIEWS

Eat Like a Local- Sarasota: Sarasota Florida Food Guide

I have lived in the Sarasota area since 1998 and learned about many great places that I want to try. –Conoal

Eat Like a Local: Connecticut: Connecticut Food Guide

This a great guide to try different places in Connecticut to eat. Can’t wait to try them all! The author is awesome to explore and try all these different foods/drinks. There are places I didn’t know they existed until I got this book and I am a CT resident myself! –Caroline J. H.

Eat Like a Local: Las Vegas: Las Vegas Nevada Food Guide

Perfect food guide for any tourist traveling to Vegas or any local looking to go outside their comfort zone! – TheBondes

Eat Like a Local-Jacksonville: Jacksonville Florida Food Guide

Loved the recommendations. Great book from someone who knows their way around Jacksonville. –Anonymous

Eat Like a Local- Costa Brava: Costa Brava Spain Food Guide

The book was very well written. Visited a few of the restaurants in the book, they were great! Sylvia V.

Eat Like a Local-Sacramento: Sacramento California Food Guide

As a native of Sacramento, Emerald's book touches on some of our areas premier spots for food and fun. She skims the surface of what Sacramento has to offer recommending locations in historical, popular areas where even more jewels can be found. –Katherine G.

EAT LIKE A LOCAL- JOHANNESBURG

Johannesburg South Africa Food Guide

Melinda Copeland

Eat Like a Local- Johannesburg Copyright © 2023 by CZYK Publishing LLC. All Rights Reserved.

All rights reserved. No part of this book may be reproduced in any form or by any electronic or mechanical means including information storage and retrieval systems, without permission in writing from the author. The only exception is by a reviewer, who may quote short excerpts in a review.

The statements in this book are of the authors and may not be the views of CZYK Publishing.

Cover designed by: Lisa Rusczyk Ed. D.

CZYK Publishing Since 2011.
CZYKPublishing.com
Eat Like a Local

Mill Hall, PA
All rights reserved.
ISBN: 9798853479852

EAT
Like A Local

BOOK DESCRIPTION

Are you excited about planning your next trip? Do you want an edible experience? Would you like some culinary guidance from a local? If you answered yes to any of these questions, then this Eat Like a Local book is for you. Eat Like a Local - Johannesburg by Melinda Copeland offers the inside scoop on food in Johannesburg South Africa. Culinary tourism is an important aspect of any travel experience. Food has the ability to tell you a story of a destination, its landscapes, and culture on a single plate. Most food guides tell you how to eat like a tourist. Although there is nothing wrong with that, as part of the Eat Like a Local series, this book will give you a food guide from someone who has lived at your next culinary destination.

In these pages, you will discover advice on having a unique edible experience. This book will not tell you exact addresses or hours but instead will give you excitement and knowledge of food and drinks from a local that you may not find in other travel food guides.

Eat like a local. Slow down, stay in one place, and get to know the food, people, and culture. By the time you finish this book, you will be eager and prepared to travel to your next culinary destination.

OUR STORY

Traveling has always been a passion of the creator of the Eat Like a Local book series. During Lisa's travels in Malta, instead of tasting what the city offered, she ate at a large fast-food chain. However, she realized that her traveling experience would have been more fulfilling if she had experienced the best of local cuisines. Most would agree that food is one of the most important aspects of a culture. Through her travels, Lisa learned how much locals had to share with tourists, especially about food. Lisa created the Eat Like a Local book series to help connect people with locals which she discovered is a topic that locals are very passionate about sharing. So please join me and: Eat, drink, and explore like a local.

TABLE OF CONTENTS

DEDICATION

This book is dedicated to my father, John Fuller, who left Tasmania at the age of 20 to go on a holiday to visit South Africa and never returned home. He fell in love with the city of Johannesburg, met my mother Joan and the rest is history.

(John Alan Fuller Born: 3 November 1943 in Tasmania, Australia – Died: 23 February 2022 in Johannesburg, South Africa)

ABOUT THE AUTHOR

Melinda Copeland is a wife and mother who lives in Alberton, Johannesburg. Melinda has toured Europe and Australia but feels like there is no place like home. Melinda loves to spend time with her family and explore the wonderful things that Johannesburg has to offer. Being a foodie and a person who loves to try new things, she has made her way around Johannesburg for 44 years and is ready to share some of the best information and tips on where to go and what to eat when you visit Johannesburg!

Make sure to include why you are a local and your association with food culture.

Melinda Copeland Nee Fuller was born in Johannesburg in 1978. Melinda studied Journalism at Intec College when she was 20 years old. When she's not writing, she can be found spending time with her family in all the inspiring places that Johannesburg has to offer and enjoying South African cuisine. Melinda is a born and bred "Joziite" and lives with her husband, son, and two daughters.

HOW TO USE THIS BOOK

The goal of this book is to help culinary travelers either dream or experience different edible experiences by providing opinions from a local. The author has made suggestions based on their own knowledge. Please do your own research before traveling to the area in case the suggested locations are unavailable.

Travel Advisories: As a first step in planning any trip abroad, check the Travel Advisories for your intended destination.
https://travel.state.gov/content/travel/en/traveladvisories/traveladvisories.html

FROM THE PUBLISHER

Traveling can be one of the most important parts of a person's life. The anticipation and memories that you have are some of the best. As a publisher of the *Eat Like a Local*, Greater Than a Tourist, as well as the popular *50 Things to Know* book series, we strive to help you learn about new places, spark your imagination, and inspire you. Wherever you are and whatever you do I wish you safe, fun, and inspiring travel.

Lisa Rusczyk Ed. D.
CZYK Publishing

"Food has the unique ability to capture moments in time. And, when you combine food experiences while traveling, you open the door to new culinary landscapes."

Auguste Escoffier

Being a proud resident of Johannesburg, in South Africa since my birth in 1978, I am thrilled to be able to share with you the wonders of this extraordinary city and its rich cultural tapestry. Despite the occasional negative press circulating, let me assure you that Johannesburg is a captivating destination that deserves to be recognized for the beautiful city that it is.

First and foremost, let me take a moment to highlight the remarkable beauty of this country. As a resident of Johannesburg, I have been able to experience this many times. Picture yourself surrounded by breathtaking landscapes that range from rolling grasslands to majestic mountain ranges. Because Johannesburg is situated on the Highveld plateau, it is blessed with a mild climate, allowing locals and tourists year-round enjoyment of the stunning natural scenery. Our Summers are hot and dry, and our Winters are mild.

Whether you're exploring the vast savannas of nearby national parks or strolling through the city's lush gardens and parks, you'll are able to immerse yourself in South Africa's captivating beauty. It is my opinion that one cannot truly understand Johannesburg without personally experiencing its vibrant and diverse culture. This city is a melting pot of various ethnicities, each contributing to its unique traditions and customs.

As I reflect on my own experiences in this remarkable city, I cannot help but feel an overwhelming sense of pride. Johannesburg has transformed itself into a vibrant metropolis, overcoming its past challenges and emerging as a beacon of hope and resilience. Its growth and development are truly inspiring.

From the moment you set foot in Johannesburg, you'll be embraced by the warm hospitality of its people, fondly known as Joziites, who are as diverse as the city itself. If you take a stroll through the bustling neighborhoods, you will most certainly witness a variety of languages, art, music, and dance that reflects the true essence of Johannesburg.

I would like to touch on the irresistible flavors that make South African cuisine a culinary adventure like no other. Johannesburg is a food lover's paradise, offering a delightful fusion of traditional African dishes, European influences, and vibrant street food culture.

Prepare your taste buds for, one of my favorites, a mouthwatering braai (barbecue) feast, savory bobotie (a spiced meat dish), fragrant bunny chows (a South African Indian specialty), and biltong (a dried meat snack that is quintessentially South African). And don't forget to pair these delectable dishes with a glass of locally produced wine or a refreshing Castle Lager, a renowned South African beer. I will delve deeper into the cuisine in Johannesburg as we continue.

Besides the culinary delights, Johannesburg boasts a lively nightlife scene, with a plethora of trendy bars, jazz clubs, and live music venues where you can dance the night away to the rhythm of African beats. Or, if you are like me and would rather have a quieter experience then you should visit the city's art galleries and museums, which showcase both contemporary and traditional African art, offering a glimpse into the rich cultural heritage of Johannesburg.

So, whether you're planning a visit or simply dreaming of the day when you'll set foot in this beautiful city, I assure you that you are in for an unforgettable journey. You will be enchanted by its natural beauty, while you embrace the diverse culture, and savor the flavors that only this city can offer. Johannesburg, my home, stands tall, a testament to the indomitable spirit of its people. I hope you will find these tips useful and learn to love Johannesburg, its people, and its cuisine as much as I do.

Johannesburg
South Africa

Johannesburg South Africa Climate

	High	Low
January	78	58
February	78	58
March	76	55
April	71	49
May	68	42
June	63	37
July	63	36
August	68	40
September	76	47
October	77	51
November	77	54
December	79	57

GreaterThanaTourist.com

Temperatures are in Fahrenheit degrees.
Source: NOAA

1. DO SOME RESEARCH

Did you know that Johannesburg shines as one of the most fascinating destinations in the world? As the largest city in South Africa, Johannesburg effortlessly blends the old and the new, offering a vibrant urban landscape intertwined with rich history and cultural heritage. I thought I would start the beginning section of this book with one of the more practical tips. Before visiting Johannesburg, it is a good idea to do some research.

The reason I say this is that there is so much to do, from exploring the poignant exhibits at the Apartheid Museum to immersing yourself in the energetic atmosphere of Soweto, Johannesburg offers a captivating blend of experiences that will leave you in awe on occasion. The problem is time. If you are only here for a short while, it would be a good idea to do some research and create an itinerary of places that you would like to visit.

I would suggest joining a food tour. This is an excellent way to delve deeper into the vibrant culinary scene of Johannesburg. Having been on many of these guided tours I can attest to the fact that you will be taken on a wonderful adventure, introducing you to a variety of local dishes, street food, and hidden gems. You'll have the opportunity to taste authentic flavors, learn about the city's food history, and interact with passionate food vendors and chefs who can share fascinating stories behind the dishes that they prepare. I can assure you that it is a fun and immersive experience that will leave you with a satisfied palate and a deeper appreciation for Johannesburg's cuisine!

Another way to get yourself accustomed to the Johannesburg vibe is to research the multitude of vibrant markets where you can explore a treasure trove of culinary delights. Some well-known Markets are The Neighbourgoods Market in Braamfontein and the Market on Main in Maboneng. Both markets offer a feast for the senses, with an array of food stalls and vendors showcasing diverse cuisines. From local favorites to international treats, you'll find everything from cheeses to fresh produce and mouthwatering street food.

It is a good idea to Google food festivals and events happening in Johannesburg throughout the year before you decide when to visit. These gatherings celebrate the city's culinary diversity and offer a fantastic opportunity to try a wide range of dishes in one place. There's always something for everyone, from wine festivals to food truck extravaganzas.

In short, Johannesburg's cuisine is a fusion of cultures and flavors, so don't hesitate to step out of your comfort zone and try something new. When I was younger, I was extremely hesitant to try different types of cuisine, but I learned very quickly to be open to the diverse culinary experiences this city has to offer. Trust me, you will be rewarded with a delectable journey that will leave your taste buds longing for more.

2. NO ELECTRICITY: NO PROBLEM

So, first things first, when you are googling Johannesburg, you are more than likely going to find many mentions of “load shedding”. Let me shed some light (pun intended) on this peculiar phenomenon and help you navigate it with a smile on your face.

First off, if you didn’t know, load shedding is when the electricity supply is temporarily cut off in certain areas due to high demand surpassing the available power. It can be a bit frustrating, but fear not, for I have some tips to make your vacation in Johannesburg as bright as ever, even when the lights go out!

First things first, always stay prepared. Keep a portable power bank handy to juice up your devices on the go. Trust me, this little savior can be a lifesaver when your phone decides to play dead just when you need it most.

Next, embrace the adventure! Treat load shedding as a unique opportunity to immerse yourself in the local culture. When the lights dim, the city comes alive with candlelit dinners, rooftop stargazing, and the warm glow of community spirit. It's like stepping into a romantic movie scene, with a dash of rustic charm thrown in! As a family, we use load shedding to fire up the braai and spend some quality time together, so either way you cannot go wrong!

If you're staying at a hotel, make sure to inquire about their backup power arrangements. Most establishments in Johannesburg have generators to keep the lights on during load shedding. Also, check if they have a bar or lounge area with backup power. It's a win-win situation – you get to enjoy a refreshing drink while the rest of the city is in darkness.

Now, let's talk about timing. Load shedding follows a schedule, which means you can plan your day around it. Check online for the updated load-shedding timetable and arrange your activities accordingly. This way, you can ensure that you're out and about when the lights decide to take a break.

Try to embrace the local lingo. Load shedding is a topic of conversation among locals, so use it as an opportunity to strike up a chat and learn more about the city from those who know it best. You might even score some insider tips on hidden gems or alternative attractions that thrive during power outages.

Basically, what I am trying to say is, don't let load-shedding dim your enthusiasm. Instead, let it be a shining moment of flexibility, creativity, and discovery. Embrace the unexpected, make the most of the candlelit ambiance, and create memories that will sparkle long after the lights come back on. Johannesburg awaits, load shedding and all!

3. THE GREAT JOHANNESBURG "BRAAI"

Ah, the Johannesburg braai. Prepare your taste buds for a mouthwatering journey through the flavors of this beloved South African tradition. Picture this: the aroma of sizzling meat, the crackling of the fire, and the sound of laughter filling the air. Welcome to the ultimate social gathering where food takes center stage! As a local, my family enjoys a braai on the patio at least once a week.

Now, let's dive into the delightful spread you'll find at a typical Johannesburg braai. At its heart, a braai is all about meat, glorious meat! We're talking succulent boerewors (sausages), tender lamb chops, juicy steaks (my personal favorite), and chicken kebabs that'll make your taste buds sing. The carnivorous feast is complemented by a variety of vibrant salads, from crunchy coleslaw to tangy potato salad, and refreshing green salads with a burst of flavors. Don't forget to load up your plate with some chakalaka, a spicy vegetable relish that adds that extra kick.

Now, when it comes to the braai itself, there are two main contenders: the charcoal braai and the gas braai. The charcoal braai, my husband's first and only choice, is the classic choice, where the charcoal is meticulously arranged, ignited, and fanned until it reaches the perfect temperature for grilling. The smoky aroma that wafts through the air adds an irresistible touch to the food. To us locals it can accurately be described as the smell of home.

On the other hand, a gas braai offers convenience and speed. With just a twist of a knob, you can have an instant flame ready to grill your meat to perfection. It's the ideal choice for those who prefer a fuss-free braai experience without compromising on taste.

I would like to touch on the magic of a braai when it comes to forging connections. A braai is more than just a meal; it's a cultural gathering that brings people from different walks of life together. Whether you're a local or a visitor, a braai is a perfect opportunity to strike up conversations, share stories, and create lasting memories. A braai is where those cultures intertwine, creating a vibrant tapestry of shared experiences and newfound friendships.

When it comes to finding the perfect spot for a braai in Johannesburg as a tourist, the options are endless. The city boasts beautiful lakeside parks like Emmarentia Dam and one of my personal favorites, Zoo Lake, where you can set up your braai station amidst nature's splendors. These serene settings offer the perfect backdrop for a relaxed afternoon of grilling and chilling.

If you're seeking a livelier atmosphere, head to the popular Braamfontein area or the vibrant Neighbourgoods Market. These bustling urban hubs provide a dynamic backdrop for your braai adventure, with a mix of food stalls, live music, and a diverse crowd that's ready to embrace the joy of a shared meal.

So, grab your tongs, fire up the grill, and let the Johannesburg braai experience ignite your senses. Discover the flavors, embrace the camaraderie, and celebrate the beauty of this cherished tradition. In Johannesburg, a braai is more than just a meal – it's a celebration of life, community, and the simple joys that bring us all together. As locals, we have forged some amazing lifelong friendships at the center of the braai.

4. WHAT TO DRINK IN JOHANNESBURG

What to drink in Johannesburg. Where do I even begin? Johannesburg offers a variety of unique and refreshing drinks. From the tantalizing flavors of alcoholic beverages to the vibrant non-alcoholic concoctions, be sure to take a sip into the world of Johannesburg beverages.

Let's start with a classic South African gem: Rooibos. Known as the "red bush tea," Rooibos is a caffeine-free herbal tea that boasts a rich, earthy flavor. It's not only delicious but also packed with antioxidants. You can find this delightful tea in almost all cafes and restaurants across Johannesburg. This tea is suitable for people of all ages from babies to the elderly.

Now, let's move on to something a little stronger, shall we? In the world of alcoholic beverages, the city of Johannesburg has a few tricks up its sleeve. First, we have Amarula, a creamy liqueur made from the marula fruit. This deliciously smooth drink has hints of caramel and vanilla, and it's best enjoyed on the rocks or as a key ingredient in cocktails. You can find Amarula in bars and liquor stores everywhere!

Another popular alcoholic beverage in South Africa is the renowned Pinotage wine. This unique wine varietal was born right here in South Africa, a cross between Pinot Noir and Cinsaut grapes. Known for its bold flavors and hints of dark berries and smokiness, Pinotage is a must-try for wine enthusiasts. This is one of my personal favorites and goes perfectly with a thick juicy steak!

For those looking for a non-alcoholic thirst quencher, Johannesburg has you covered. Don't miss out on the iconic "Ginger Beer," a spicy and effervescent beverage that packs a punch. You can find this fiery delight in various locations, including local markets like the Neighbourgoods Market.

Lastly, if you're feeling adventurous, indulge in a uniquely South African soft drink called "Sparberry." This bright red, raspberry-flavored soda is like a party in your mouth. It's a nostalgic favorite among the people of Johannesburg and can be found in many local supermarkets and convenience stores across the city. Trust me, the kids will love it!

5. PLACES TO SHOP

Contrary to popular belief, Johannesburg has hundreds of beautiful shopping malls. Step into a world of retail wonder, where shopping centers beckon with their architectural splendor and a treasure trove of stores. Having been to nearly all these malls, allow me to take you on a journey through some of the city's stunning shopping destinations that showcase both style and substance.

A firm favorite amongst the residents of Johannesburg can be found in Sandton! Prepare to be dazzled by the grandeur of Sandton City, a premier shopping center that epitomizes luxury and sophistication. With its towering glass façade and elegant interior, it's a sight to behold. Stroll through its gleaming halls adorned with designer boutiques, international brands, and upscale retailers. The beautifully curated spaces create an atmosphere of opulence, while the skylights flood the center with natural light, adding a touch of glamour to your shopping experience.

As its name suggests, the Mall of Africa is a shopping extravaganza on a grand scale. This architectural marvel boasts a striking contemporary design that captures the imagination. The mall's sleek façade and expansive interiors create a sense of awe as you explore its vast array of shops. With over 300 stores offering everything from fashion to homeware, it's a shopper's paradise where you can indulge in retail therapy amidst an atmosphere of modern elegance. Trust me, whatever you are looking for you are going to find it in this mall!

At the center of the upscale suburb of Hyde Park, Hyde Park Corner exudes an air of refinement and sophistication. This shopping center presents a harmonious blend of contemporary architecture and landscaped gardens. Its sleek lines and stylish interior provide an inviting ambiance for discerning shoppers. Discover a curated collection of high-end boutiques, exclusive fashion brands, and upscale dining options. As you wander through its polished halls, you'll feel a sense of timeless elegance that adds an extra layer of allure to your shopping experience.

One of the oldest malls in Johannesburg and boasting a distinctive design inspired by the iconic

Acropolis in Athens, Eastgate Shopping Centre is a true architectural gem. This mall brings back many memories for me, as it was a place where everyone would meet to hang out after school. Its majestic entrance, adorned with grand pillars and classical elements, sets the stage for a shopping journey like no other. Once you have stepped inside, you will find a vast selection of local and international brands, fashion-forward stores, and enticing dining options. This is what memories are made of.

Prepare to be captivated by the charm of Melrose Arch, a vibrant urban precinct that seamlessly combines shopping, dining, and entertainment. This pedestrian-friendly space features European-inspired architecture with beautifully designed piazzas and charming walkways lined with stylish boutiques and chic cafes. The blend of contemporary and classical elements creates a visually stunning environment that invites you to indulge in a leisurely shopping experience amidst a lively atmosphere.

If you are looking to immerse yourself in a treasure trove of unique finds and local craftsmanship, there's something for everyone in the City of Gold. In my opinion, you cannot leave Johannesburg if you haven't experienced the magic of one of our unique craft markets.

One of your first stops should be the Neighbourgoods Market located in the trendy Braamfontein area. This market is a treasure of local creativity. It features a wide range of stalls offering artisanal foods, handcrafted goods, vintage clothing, and unique artwork, some of which are hung up in my own living room. Also, remember to look out for Jozi Blue for handmade leather products or grab a bite from the array of gourmet food vendors.

Secondly, we have The Market on Main takes place every Sunday in the Maboneng Precinct. This market is a gathering of local designers, artisans, and food vendors, a perfect mix for a good day out. You can browse through stalls showcasing fashion, accessories, home décor, and organic produce.

Next up, we have The African Craft Market, situated in Rosebank Mall. This market is filled with African craftsmanship and offers a vast selection of traditional crafts, including intricate beadwork, wood carvings, woven baskets, and vibrant textiles. This is the perfect market to find something to take home a piece of African heritage.

The Maboneng Precinct in Maboneng is widely known for its artistic flair, Maboneng is home to numerous boutique shops and art galleries. One must-visit store is Love Jozi, where you can find unique T-shirts, accessories, and artwork inspired by the city. Another gem is "I Was Shot in Joburg", which sells photography prints captured by underprivileged youth.

If you have a passion for books, then why not visit the Bamboo Lifestyle Centre. This center is in Melville and focuses on sustainable and locally made products. Here you can find stores like The Bamboo Farmer, offering eco-friendly household items, or Enchantrix Books and Collectibles which is an absolute haven for book lovers.

Finally, one of my personal favorites, the Rosebank Sunday Rooftop Market. This market is held on the rooftop of Rosebank Mall and is a delightful mix of crafts, clothing, accessories, and delicious street food. Here you can purchase some unique fashion at the Kafui Naturals Boutique or browse through handmade leather goods at Wild Leather.

These are just a few examples of the diverse shopping centers, craft markets, and unique shops you can find in Johannesburg. So, put on your shopping shoes, embrace the Johannesburg atmosphere, and explore the delightful world of Johannesburg's shopping scene.

So, here's a cool thing about shopping in Johannesburg. Bargaining is part of the game. Yep, you heard it right! Don't be shy to negotiate prices, especially in markets or smaller shops. The vendors expect it, and it can be quite an adventure. Just remember to keep it friendly and have an idea of the price range you're comfortable with. Who knows, you might just score an amazing deal!

Now, I know shopping is exciting, but safety should always be a priority. Stick to well-lit and crowded areas, especially when exploring the city center. Keep an eye on your belongings and avoid displaying expensive items or carrying large amounts of cash.

6. NAVIGATING THE CITY

So, when it comes to navigating the city of Johannesburg, there are a few tips and tricks that can help you get around the city smoothly.

First things first, make sure you have a reliable map app on your phone. Apps like Google Maps or Waze are super handy for finding your way around the city streets. They'll give you the best routes to your destination and help you avoid any unexpected detours. As a local to the city, there are times that even I have had to make use of these apps as there are just so many places that I have still yet to see myself.

Now, when it comes to getting from point A to point B, one of the most popular options for both locals and tourists is Uber. This is one of the safest and most convenient ways to travel around Johannesburg. Just download the Uber app, set up your account, and you'll be able to request a ride with ease.

Another great option, especially if you're looking to travel longer distances, is the Gautrain. The Gautrain is a modern rail system that connects different parts of the city, including the airport, Sandton, and Pretoria. It's fast, reliable, and comfortable, making it a preferred choice, especially during peak hours when the roads can get congested. When you step on board, you'll notice the modern and comfy seating arrangements. They've got air conditioning too, so even on those scorching hot days, you can sit back and relax in a cool and pleasant environment.

As you ride the Gautrain, you'll be treated to some beautiful sights of Johannesburg. You'll see the city skyline, lush greenery, and vibrant neighborhoods passing by. It's a great way to take in the sights and enjoy the unique perspective that the train offers. As locals, we have made use of the Gautrain to spend quality time with the family and experience the views from this famous train.

Of course, while you're out and about in Johannesburg, as with any foreign country, it's important to stay aware of your surroundings. Keep your belongings secure and avoid flashing any expensive items. It's always a good idea to stick to well-lit and populated areas, especially at night.

Planning your route in advance can also save you some time and stress. Johannesburg is a big city, and traffic can be unpredictable. So, check your map app for estimated travel times and keep in mind any potential delays due to rush hour or road closures.

7. THE BEST TIME TO VISIT

If you're planning a visit, you might be wondering when the best time is to experience all that this vibrant city has to offer. In my honest opinion, Spring, Summer, Autumn, and Winter are all the perfect times to visit Johannesburg!

Summers in Johannesburg can be quite a scorcher, but luckily Johannesburg Summers are not humid, making this season the perfect time to explore the city's outdoor attractions and enjoy some serious fun in the sun. It's the perfect opportunity to sample local delicacies, pick up unique souvenirs, and soak up the infectious energy of Johannesburg.

Summer is also the time for thrilling outdoor adventures. Johannesburg is surrounded by breathtaking natural landscapes, and the summer months are ideal for hiking, biking, or even embarking on a safari adventure. Remember to slap on some sunscreen, grab your safari hat, and get ready to explore the wild side of Johannesburg.

Lest I forget to mention the stunning parks and gardens that come alive during the summer months. If you decide to take a walk through the Johannesburg Botanical Garden, you will be greeted by a riot of colors and fragrances. Pack a picnic, find a shady spot, and enjoy a lazy afternoon surrounded by nature's beauty. Just be sure to have some bug spray handy to keep those pesky critters at bay, especially during the summer months.

Now, Winters in Johannesburg might not be as cold as the North Pole, but hey, it's still winter! Don't worry, though; the city has plenty to offer even when the temperatures drop.

Winter is the time when the city of Johannesburg comes alive with theater performances, art exhibitions, and music festivals that will warm your soul. I strongly advise watching a show at the iconic Market Theatre or perhaps exploring the galleries of the Maboneng Precinct. You won’t be sorry!

If you're a history buff, Johannesburg's museums will transport you back in time. The Apartheid Museum will give you a powerful journey through South Africa's complex past. And for some lighthearted fun, don't miss the quirky exhibits at the James Hall Museum of Transport. I remember spotting a vintage car there that made me turn to my husband and say, "Wow, I didn't know they made cars that way!"

I find Winter to be the perfect time to indulge in the city's culinary delights, which are many! Johannesburg boasts a thriving food scene with diverse cuisines from around the world. It is the perfect opportunity to tuck into a steaming bowl of comforting soup or warm up with a cup of rich hot chocolate at one of the trendy cafes in the city. Who needs a fireplace if you can warm up from the inside out?

And let's not forget shopping as I talked about earlier! Winter is the perfect time to unleash your inner shopaholic while visiting Johannesburg. With so many shopping centers and craft markets out there, you are quite literally spoilt for choice!

So, whether you're basking in the summer sun or braving the winter chill, Johannesburg has something to offer every adventurous traveler. Embrace the seasons, soak up the culture, and let this city of gold leave you with memories that shine brighter than, well, actual gold!

8. FEEL LIKE ROYALTY

I would like to talk about some of the superior hotels in Johannesburg, where luxury knows no boundaries! There are two iconic establishments that will make your stay in the city simply extraordinary. Unfortunately, I have not had the pleasure of staying in one of these hotels myself, but I have visited friends who were staying at the Saxon Hotel while visiting from Australia, and staying in that hotel for a night is now on my bucket list!

You will be swept off your feet by the sheer elegance and opulence of this magnificent hotel. As soon as you step into the grand entrance, you're enveloped in an ambiance of refined luxury. The Saxon's rooms are a true haven of comfort, tastefully designed with attention to every detail. This hotel also offers picture-perfect views of the cityscape from your window. It does not come cheap, but if you are planning to visit Johannesburg this hotel will truly leave you mesmerized.

I have, however, had the experience of dining at The Saxon Hotel. This experience will take dining to a whole new level. At the Qunu Restaurant, you will be able to indulge in the finest meals, where talented chefs create masterpieces on a plate. From international cuisine to a fusion of flavors inspired by South Africa's rich culinary heritage, every dish is crafted with precision and passion. Qunu offers a menu that features traditional South African dishes with a modern twist, prepared using the freshest locally sourced ingredients. Don't forget to pair your meal with a carefully selected wine from their extensive cellar—it's a match made in gourmet heaven!

When it comes to activities, The Saxon offers a wealth of options to cater to your every desire. You can immerse yourself in pure bliss at their world-class spa, where skilled therapists will pamper you with indulgent treatments and soothing massages. If, however, you are feeling more energetic, you can take a refreshing dip in their sparkling pool or work up a sweat at the state-of-the-art fitness center.

Next up, we have The Michelangelo Hotel. I have never set foot in this hotel, as quite honestly, I may never want to leave. This hotel is a true gem nestled in the suburb of Sandton, which is one of Johannesburg's most bustling business and shopping districts. The Michelangelo offers a range of impeccably designed rooms, each providing a haven of tranquility amidst the urban bustle. And oh, the views! Gaze out from your window to witness the breathtaking city skyline which is a sight that will make you feel like you're on top of the world. I have seen pictures on their website, and they are beyond amazing!

The Michelangelo Hotel is well known for its spectacular culinary offerings and is a haven for culinary enthusiasts. This hotel offers sumptuous buffets that have an array of international delicacies and fine dining experiences. You will be able to sample the freshest local ingredients and savor exquisite flavors that will leave you wanting more. And don't forget to complement your dining experience with a glass of fine South African wine!

When it comes to activities, the Michelangelo is in an ideal location to explore the surroundings. You will be able to take a stroll through Nelson Mandela Square, which is located nearby, where you'll find a variety of shops and cafes. If relaxation is more your style, then you can head to the hotel's tranquil spa and indulge in rejuvenating treatments that will leave you feeling refreshed and revitalized.

Both The Saxon Hotel and The Michelangelo Hotel are known to exude a level of elegance and luxury that is simply unmatched. Their meticulous attention to detail, impeccable service, and stunning design elements creates an unforgettable experience for every guest. Whether you choose the refined tranquility of The Saxon or the urban chic of The Michelangelo, rest assured that your stay will be nothing short of extraordinary.

9. DRESS FOR THE OCCASION

I know that when I visit a foreign country there must be at least one night when I am able to dress up! Let's talk about a few incredible venues in Johannesburg where dressing up for dinner is an absolute must! These places not only offer exceptional cuisine but also create an atmosphere of elegance and sophistication that will make your dining experience truly memorable.

If it is a spectacular view that you are looking for then you must visit the View Restaurant at the Four Seasons Hotel. This restaurant offers not only exquisite food but also panoramic views that will take your breath away. The city skyline is visible through the floor-to-ceiling windows and the culinary offerings at are a fusion of international flavors with a South African touch. Choose from dishes such as seared scallops, succulent lamb, and a range of delectable desserts. This restaurant is certainly a good reason to get dressed up!

If you're looking for a truly unique and innovative dining experience, The Test Kitchen is the place to go.

This establishment is situated in the hip neighborhood of Woodstock and pushes the boundaries of culinary creativity. The Test Kitchen offers a multi-course tasting menu that will tantalize your senses. You will be amazed by dishes that are as visually stunning as they are delicious, showcasing a blend of flavors and techniques. They also have a lively cocktail bar and a well-curated wine cellar to add an extra touch of excitement to your evening.

For those like me who are seeking a tranquil and indulgent dining experience, Mosaic at The Orient is the perfect choice. Nestled in the peaceful suburb of Elandsfontein, this hidden gem offers a luxurious setting and a culinary journey like no other. This elegant boutique hotel restaurant offers the most exquisite flavors in their dishes combining local and international influences. Each plate at Mosaic is a work of art, meticulously prepared with a focus on presentation and taste. Take pictures of your food! I do this every time I go there.

I am now going to tell you about a unique venue in Johannesburg where dining becomes an extraordinary experience, and fancy dress is part of the magic! If you want to dress up, and I mean really dress up then

Greensleeves Medieval Kingdom is the place to do it. Greensleeves encompasses the era of knights, maidens, and royal feasts. And don't worry about finding an outfit beforehand if you don't want to as they offer an array of outfits to try on and wear before you enter the restaurant.

As you step into Greensleeves, you'll find yourself immersed in a medieval wonderland. The venue is adorned with lavish decorations, creating an atmosphere reminiscent of a medieval castle.

Now, let's talk about the food, fit for royalty! At Greensleeves, you'll be treated to a traditional medieval feast that will satisfy even the heartiest of appetites. The tables are adorned with hearty platters filled with succulent roast meats, delectable game dishes, and an array of seasonal vegetables. I personally love this venue and have been to it many times. I have pictures of myself and some friends indulging in a feast fit for a king or queen, feasting with our hands, and savoring the flavors of a bygone era. There are vegetarian options available too, ensuring that everyone can partake in the medieval festivities.

But dining at Greensleeves is not just about the food—it's an immersive experience that transports you to medieval times. Throughout the evening, you'll be entertained by jesters, troubadours, and medieval musicians, providing a delightful backdrop of merriment. Witness exciting sword-fighting displays, marvel at mesmerizing fire performances, and be captivated by traditional dances. It's like stepping into a medieval fairytale, where every moment is filled with enchantment. I can assure you, plenty of memories will be made at Greensleeves!

These remarkable venues in Johannesburg offer not only incredible food but also an enchanting atmosphere and additional activities that go beyond just dining. So, dress your best, indulge in culinary delights, and let these exquisite establishments transport you to a world of elegance and food!

10. GROCERIES AND BRANDS UNIQUE TO JOHANNESBURG

When it comes to buying groceries in Johannesburg, you'll find a wide range of options that cater to all tastes and preferences. From local supermarkets to specialized stores, the city offers a diverse shopping experience that ensures you'll find everything you need to satisfy your culinary desires.

I want to start with the major supermarket chains that are popular in Johannesburg. One of the leading names is Pick n Pay, a well-known retailer that offers a comprehensive selection of groceries, fresh produce, and household essentials. With numerous branches across the city, Pick n Pay provides convenience and quality at affordable prices. They stock both local and international brands, making it a go-to destination for everyday shopping needs.

Another prominent supermarket chain is Checkers, which prides itself on offering quality products with a focus on fresh produce, gourmet ingredients, and specialty items. Checkers often partners with renowned chefs and local producers to offer unique and premium food options. It's a great place to find high-quality meats, cheeses, and artisanal products that will elevate your culinary adventures in Johannesburg. The one thing I love about Checkers is that they have a highly efficient delivery service called Checkers 360. Simply download the app, have your groceries delivered and voila, you don't even need to leave your room!

For those seeking a premium shopping experience, Woolworths is a top choice. This retailer is synonymous with quality and offers an extensive range of organic, free-range, and sustainable products. From fresh produce to ready-made meals and gourmet treats, you'll find a wide array of premium products that are perfect for those looking for something special. Woolworths is a little more expensive than other supermarkets, but their quality cannot be beaten.

Don't forget that you can also get groceries at The Neighbourgoods Market and Market on Main. These markets showcase a plethora of local produce, artisanal products, and street food delicacies. These markets give you the opportunity to discover unique flavors and interact with local vendors.

My sister moved to Australia a few years ago and constantly complains that they are not able to find some of her favorite brands in their local supermarkets. The reason for this is that in Johannesburg there are a lot of products that are unique to this country and may not be readily available in tourists' home countries. So, why not try them while you are here visiting?

Biltong, a favorite that never lasts long on our house, for example, is a beloved South African specialty that visitors absolutely must try. It's a form of cured and dried meat, typically beef or game, that is seasoned with a blend of spices and air-dried to perfection. Beware though, it is addictive!

Another South African favorite is Rooibos tea. This tea can be found in most Johannesburg households and is derived from the indigenous Rooibos plant, this herbal tea is renowned for its distinct flavor and health benefits. It's caffeine-free, packed with antioxidants, and has a naturally sweet and earthy taste. Rooibos tea is a must-try for tea enthusiasts and a great souvenir to bring back home.

Mrs. Balls Chutney is another absolute classic. This iconic fruity and spicy chutney has been a staple in

South African households for over a century. It pairs perfectly with a variety of dishes, from traditional braais (barbecues) to sandwiches and curries. A jar of Mrs. Balls Chutney is a delightful addition to any pantry and a taste of South African culinary heritage.

If you have a sweet tooth, be sure to try Ouma Rusks. These delicious, crunchy biscuit-like treats are a beloved South African tradition that have long been a part of my family's daily lives. They're perfect for dipping into your morning coffee or tea, and they come in various flavors, such as buttermilk, condensed milk, and muesli. Ouma Rusks are a delightful snack that captures the essence of South African comfort food.

Do you feel like a beer that is uniquely South African? Castle Lager is a popular choice among beer enthusiasts. This beer has been brewed since 1895 and offers a refreshing and crisp taste that pairs well with South African braais and social gatherings. It's a must-try for those looking to experience the local beer culture at any braai or get together.

Johannesburg is also home to a myriad of specialty stores and gourmet delis that offer a wide selection of artisanal products, organic produce, and imported delicacies. Places like Braeside Meat Market, Jackson's Real Food Market, and Cheese Gourmet are just a few examples of the specialized retailers that cater to discerning palates and those seeking unique culinary experiences.

So, whether you're shopping at major supermarket chains, exploring local markets, or seeking out specialty stores, buying groceries in Johannesburg is a delightful experience. You'll have access to a wide range of brands, local and international, and the opportunity to discover unique South African products that will add a touch of excitement and authenticity to your culinary journey.

11. LEARNING THE JOHANNESBURG LINGO

Alright, so let’s dive into the fascinating world of Johannesburg lingo! This city has its own unique vocabulary, filled with vibrant expressions and colorful slang that will make you feel like a true Jozi local. And let me tell you, learning a bit of the local lingo can be a total game-changer for tourists. Not only will it help you navigate the city with ease, but it'll also make you feel like you are part of the Jozi tribe. Learning the Jozi Lingo is not a must, but it is a lot of fun!

First things first, let's talk about one of the most common phrases you'll hear: "Howzit?" This is the ultimate Jozi greeting, equivalent to "How are you?" But here's the thing—it's not just a simple question. It's a way of saying "Hello" with a touch of casual coolness. So, when you walk the streets of Johannesburg, channel your inner Joburger and greet everyone you meet with a cheery "Howzit?" Trust me, it's an instant icebreaker and a surefire way to blend in with the locals.

Here is a very important one to remember! In Johannesburg, when someone invites you to a social gathering or a party, they'll most likely say, "Hey, come join us for a dop." Now, you might be thinking, "What on earth is a dop?" Well, my friend, a dop is a good old-fashioned alcoholic beverage. So, next time you're invited for a dop, don't be shy—raise your glass and join in the fun!

Here is a phrase that will come in handy when exploring markets and streets of Johannesburg: "Eish!" This versatile expression can be used to convey surprise, frustration, or even admiration. So, when you stumble upon a fantastic find at a market stall, exclaim, "Eish, this is amazing!" Or if you encounter unexpected traffic on your way to an attraction, let out a cheeky "Eish, this is not on!" Trust me, it's a surefire way to connect with the locals and show that you're in on the Jozi lingo.

Now, when it comes to food, Johannesburg has its own mouthwatering vocabulary. Picture yourself at a local eatery, perusing the menu. Instead of saying, "I'll have a hamburger," why not add a touch of Jozi flair and say, "I'll have a lekker burger, please!" "Lekker" is a popular Afrikaans word that means "delicious" or "great,". Using it will not only make your taste buds tingle but also earn you extra points with the locals.

And speaking of Afrikaans, let's explore some common phrases that will make you feel like a true local in no time. When someone asks you how you're doing, why not respond with a cheeky "Lekker, bru!" or "Sharp, my china!" "Bru" is short for "brother" and "china" is derived from the Cockney rhyming slang "china plate," meaning "mate." These phrases add a touch of warmth and familiarity to your conversations, instantly connecting you with the spirit of Johannesburg. As a local, if you don't use these phrases then you are not truly a local!

Learning the lingo of Johannesburg isn't just about the words—it's about immersing yourself in the city's vibrant culture and connecting with its people on a deeper level. When you speak the local language, even if it's just a few phrases, you open doors to genuine interactions and laughter-filled conversations. Locals will appreciate your effort to embrace their lingo and will be more than happy to share their favorite spots, hidden gems, and insider tips.

12. HOW TO TIP

Ah, tipping in Johannesburg—a topic that can sometimes leave visitors scratching their heads and wondering about the appropriate etiquette. But fear not, for I am here to guide you through the art of tipping in this vibrant city!

Let's start with waiters and waitresses, those hardworking individuals who ensure you have a delightful dining experience. It is important to remember that for many of these staff, tips can be the only substantial amount of money that they will make for their shift. So, when dining at a restaurant in Johannesburg, it's customary to leave a tip for your server as a token of appreciation for their service. Now, the question is, how much should you tip?

As a rule, and what I normally do, is give a tip of around 10-15% of the total bill is considered a fair and generous gesture. However, keep in mind that tipping is ultimately discretionary, and you can adjust the amount based on the quality of service you received. If you had an exceptional dining experience with attentive and friendly service, feel free to be a bit more generous with your tip—it's a wonderful way to show your gratitude and acknowledge their efforts in making your meal enjoyable.

Now, let's move on to car guards. If you haven't yet heard of a car guard, you will soon come to learn that they are an integral part of Johannesburg's urban landscape. These friendly individuals assist with parking your vehicle and keeping an eye on it while you go about your business. It's customary to give a small tip to the car guard as a gesture of appreciation for their service. This can vary depending on the length of time they've watched over your car and the location. You can typically hand them a few Rand coins, whatever you feel comfortable giving. Remember, these car guards work hard to ensure the safety of your vehicle and it is often their only income, so a little token of gratitude goes a long way.

When it comes to other service providers, such as hotel staff, tour guides, or taxi drivers, tipping is also customary. Hotel staff, including porters who assist with your luggage, can be tipped around 10-20 Rand per bag or more, depending on the level of service. These individuals often go the extra mile to make your stay comfortable, so it's nice to show your appreciation for their efforts.

Remember that tipping is a gesture of appreciation and not an obligation. It's always at your discretion, based on the level of service you receive and your personal satisfaction. If someone's service falls short of your expectations, it's okay to adjust the tip accordingly or provide constructive feedback instead.

When it comes to tipping, it's best to have some small denomination notes and coins on hand. This makes it easier to give the exact amount or to round up the nearest convenient tip. It's also a good idea to keep a separate envelope or a small container in your bag or pocket for organizing your tips, making it more convenient to access and distribute them when needed, especially if you are a tourist and still coming to grips with the whole car guard tipping thing!

13. AMUSEMENT PARKS

So, where do you go when you are the kids are looking for a thrilling adventure through the amusement parks of Johannesburg! Whether you're a kid at heart or have little ones in tow, these parks offer a world of fun and excitement for both adults and children.

I am going to start with Gold Reef City Theme Park, as this is a firm favorite amongst my children. This theme park is a treasure trove of excitement and entertainment. This iconic amusement park combines thrilling rides, historical attractions, and a touch of old-world charm. For adrenaline junkies, there are heart-pounding roller coasters like the Anaconda and the Tower of Terror, guaranteed to get your heart racing, not that I would know. My kids tell me.

If you're more inclined towards family-friendly fun, enjoy the gentle spins and twirls of the Antique Cars or take a leisurely ride on the Ferris wheel for panoramic views of the city. Please don't miss out on the underground mine tour. This is a unique tour that allows you to experience the rich history of Johannesburg's gold rush.

Were you told that Africa has lions walking the streets? Were you disappointed that you have not seen any yet? Truth be told, we have no wild animals walking around Johannesburg, so your best bet is to visit the popular Lion Park. As the name suggests, this park offers a unique opportunity to get up close and personal with the king of the jungle—yes, actual lions!

You will be able to take a guided safari tour through the park, where you can spot lions, cheetahs, and other magnificent African wildlife in their natural habitat. If you truly want to remember your Johannesburg visit, you must pet the lion cubs. This is of course under the supervision of experienced handlers. The Lion Park is an educational experience that teaches visitors about wildlife conservation. It's a must-visit for animal lovers and those seeking a truly unforgettable encounter with nature.

If you have decided to visit in the heart of Summer and want to beat the heat and make a splash, head to one of Johannesburg's best known water parks. Wild Waters at Boksburg has been around for many years and offers a wide array of water slides, wave pools, and lazy rivers for the ultimate aquatic adventure. Your children will be able to frolic in the shallow pools and enjoy the water play areas, while you can unwind on a tube ride or brave the exhilarating speed slides.

Unfortunately, Johannesburg is not situated near to any beaches, so if you are looking for a tropical paradise experience, visit the Valley of Waves at Sun City Resort. This water park is a veritable oasis, complete with a man-made beach, palm trees, and a wave pool that mimics the ocean's gentle swells. You can ride the waves, float along the lazy river, or take a thrilling plunge down the water slides. This is a fantastic destination for families, one that I know very well, where both adults and children can soak up the sun, enjoy the water, and relax in the lush surroundings.

Allow me to share a few tips for when you visit our famous theme and amusement parks. It’s always a good idea to check the park's website or social media channels for any updates or special events before your visit. This way, you can plan your day accordingly and make the most of your time at the park. Be aware that if there are special events happening the park will be extremely busy with drives of people. I personally prefer to go when it is less busy, but if you enjoy masses of people then by all means. Consider purchasing tickets online in advance to avoid long queues and ensure a smooth entry.

The African sun takes no prisoners so please remember to pack sunscreen, hats, and comfortable shoes for those sunny and hot days. It’s also very important to stay hydrated by bringing along water bottles or making use of the park's drinking fountains.

If you're looking to take a break from the excitement and enjoy a meal or snack, most amusement parks and water parks have dining options on-site. However, these can sometimes be pricey. I often bring along some snacks and bottled water to keep everyone fueled and hydrated throughout the day. This will also help save some money and give you the flexibility to snack whenever hunger strikes. Most importantly, don’t forget to have fun and embrace the childlike wonder that these parks evoke. Take lots of photos, create lasting memories, and enjoy every moment of your adventure. Let your inner child run wild and be sure to ride your favorite attractions as many times as you can!

14. CASINOS

Let us now look at the captivating world of casinos in Johannesburg. As a fellow traveler, I want to ensure that your visit to these magical venues is truly unforgettable. So, let's explore the mesmerizing experiences and offer some tips to enhance your time at the casinos.

Montecasino is one of Johannesburg's most iconic casinos, and while there are many others in Johannesburg, I feel that because most of my personal casino experiences have been mostly at Montecasino, this is the venue that I am able to offer you the most tips.

If you want luxury, you will find it at Montecasino. As you enter, you'll be embraced by an ambiance that transports you to a world of elegance and sophistication. The gaming floor is alive with the sounds of spinning slot machines, the cheers of winners, and the anticipation of what lies ahead. The casino offers a wide range of games to suit every taste and skill level. Whether you're a seasoned player or new to the world of gambling, you'll find something that piques your interest. You will find everything, from classic slot machines to thrilling table games like blackjack, roulette, and poker.

But there's more to this casino than just gambling. Montecasino houses the magnificent Teatro—a state-of-the-art theater that hosts awe-inspiring performances. From Broadway-style musicals to internationally acclaimed music concerts and side-splitting comedy shows, the Teatro offers a variety of entertainment options that will leave you in awe. The Teatro is a recipe for the perfect night of laughter, music, and theatrical magic while you witness the talent of world-class performers. An absolutely amazing experience!

If you have come to visit South Africa with young children, you have options when visiting Montecasino. This casino understands the importance of providing family-friendly experiences and offers a range of activities that will delight children of all ages. The Magic Company for one, is a paradise of arcade games, bumper cars, and laser tag. When you feel that it's time to unwind, you can take them to the adjacent Bird Gardens. Here, they can discover a variety of bird species, get up close to reptiles, and feed the birds.

So, here are a few more tips to make the most of your experience. Firstly, take the time to familiarize yourself with the casino's rules and regulations. Each establishment may have its own policies regarding dress code, age restrictions, and entry requirements. Some casinos may require a valid identification document, so it's best to have your ID or passport with you to avoid any inconveniences at the entrance.

Take breaks and pace yourself throughout the day. It's easy to lose track of time when you're engrossed in the gaming atmosphere. Stepping away from the gaming floor to explore the casino's restaurants and other amenities can provide a refreshing change of pace. Remember to eat! Indulge in a delicious meal at one of the fine dining establishments or savor a cocktail at one of the stylish bars.

Lastly, keep in mind that many casinos offer loyalty programs or membership cards that can enhance your experience. Consider signing up for these programs to unlock additional benefits and rewards. You may receive perks such as discounts on dining, free slot play, priority access to shows, or even exclusive invitations to special events. These programs can add an extra layer of enjoyment to your visit and make you feel like a valued guest.

15. FOR THE KIDS

If your children are anything like mine were when they were younger, you know how hard it can be to keep them occupied. Luckily, Johannesburg is a city filled with excitement and fun, offering a wide array of activities that will keep your children entertained and create memories to last a lifetime. So, let's look at the vibrant world of Johannesburg and discover the fantastic things that your little one can do to prevent themselves from feeling as my kids would say, "bored".

If your little ones are animal fanatics, then your first stop should be Johannesburg Zoo! This is a must-visit for families looking to get up close and personal with a fascinating array of animals. Your children will be captivated as they wander through the zoo, spotting lions, elephants, giraffes, and so much more.

I would suggest making the most of your visit and joining one of the guided tours or attending a feeding session where your kids can learn interesting facts about the animals and witness their feeding habits firsthand. Don't forget to pack a picnic and enjoy a leisurely lunch in the beautiful surroundings of the zoo. Alternatively, the Johannesburg Zoo Restaurant offers a refreshing dining experience amidst the natural beauty of the zoo. With a diverse menu featuring both local and international cuisine, visitors can savor delicious meals while enjoying stunning views of wildlife. It's a unique blend of food and nature.

Next on the list should be the Sci-Bono Discovery Centre. Your little ones can unleash their curiosity and dive into a world of interactive exhibits, hands-on experiments, and mind-boggling displays. There is honestly so much to do here and is perfect for inquisitive minds. Your children can explore the wonders of space, learn about the human body, and even experiment with electricity and robotics. Be sure to check the schedule for special workshops and shows that offer even more engaging experiences.

At the Sci-Bono Discovery Centre, food enthusiasts can indulge in a range of delectable options. From a variety of cuisines to grab-and-go snacks, the center's restaurants cater to diverse tastes. Whether you're craving a quick bite or a full meal, there's something for everyone.

If your children love the great outdoors, then the Walter Sisulu National Botanical Garden is the perfect destination. Here, they can run free and explore the natural beauty of the gardens. My favorite is the leisurely stroll along the winding paths that lead to an impressive waterfall. Pack a picnic and find a cozy spot under the shade of a tree, enjoying the fresh air and tranquility of nature. Don't forget to bring along a blanket if you are picnicking and as always, remember the sunscreen!

If you don't feel like packing a picnic, then you can visit their charming on-site restaurant. Here you will find a blend of culinary delights and enjoy a diverse menu of freshly prepared dishes while overlooking the serene beauty of the garden. It's the perfect spot to relax and indulge in nature's tranquility while treating your kids and your taste buds!

Now, here are a few tips to ensure a smooth and enjoyable experience for you and your children. Firstly, it's always a good idea to check the opening hours and any specific requirements for the attractions you plan to visit. Some places may require advanced bookings or have specific time slots, so it's best to plan to avoid disappointment.

When exploring outdoor spaces like the zoo or botanical garden, encourage your children to observe and appreciate the natural surroundings. Help them understand the importance of respecting the animals and plants they encounter, reminding them not to disturb or feed any animals unless specifically permitted. It's a wonderful opportunity to foster a love for nature and wildlife conservation.

Lastly, embrace the spirit of adventure and let your children's imaginations soar. Encourage them to ask questions, engage with the exhibits, and participate in interactive activities. Allow them to take the lead and follow their interests, as each child is unique in their own way. Remember, it's all about creating magical moments and cherished memories that will stay with your family long after your visit to Johannesburg.

16. CURRENCY TO CARRY

When traveling to Johannesburg, it's important to be prepared and have a good understanding of the currency used, places where you can exchange your money, and some handy tips on managing your finances while exploring Johannesburg.

The official currency of South Africa is the South African Rand (ZAR). The Rand is denoted by the symbol "R" and is subdivided into 100 cents. You'll find banknotes in denominations of R10, R20, R50, R100, and R200, while coins come in values of 1c, 2c, 5c, 10c, 20c, 50c, R1, R2, and R5. It's worth noting that while some businesses may accept major foreign currencies or credit cards, it's generally advisable to have some Rand on hand for day-to-day expenses, as you never know what may come up!

When it comes to exchanging currency, Johannesburg offers various options. One of the most convenient places to exchange your money is at the airport. This is usually my first choice when travelling to avoid having to find a bank when you are already in holiday mode!

In saying that, banks are reliable and widely available in Johannesburg, and they typically offer competitive exchange rates. You can visit a local bank branch and present your foreign currency to be exchanged for Rand. It's always a good idea to check the exchange rates beforehand and compare them with other options to ensure you're getting a fair deal. Don't forget to bring your passport or identification as it will be required for the transaction.

Now, let's talk about managing your money while in Johannesburg. It's always wise to have a combination of cash and cards to cover your expenses. Cash is essential for smaller transactions, such as street vendors and local markets that do not accept bank cards. Although, to be quite honest I have found of late that many local market vendors have credit card machines readily available.

For larger transactions or payments at established businesses, credit cards are widely accepted in Johannesburg. Visa and Mastercard are the most used cards, followed by American Express and Diners Club. I always inform your bank or credit card provider about my travel plans to ensure seamless transactions and prevent any unexpected issues with my cards when I travel.

When using ATMs in Johannesburg, I would suggest you opt for those located in well-lit and secure areas, such as inside shopping malls or near banks. Always be cautious of your surroundings and shield the keypad while entering your PIN.

As with any travel destination in the world, it's important to be vigilant with your belongings and practice general safety precautions. Keep your money, cards, and identification secure and separate them in different places. Also, try to avoid displaying large amounts of cash in public, and be aware of your surroundings when making transactions.

17. HOW JOHANNESBURG CUISINE RELATES TO OUR DIVERSE CULTURE

A cuisine like no other! As we delve into the diverse culinary landscape of Johannesburg, I'll provide you with some tips on how to navigate the cuisine and highlight a few mouthwatering dishes you must try.

Johannesburg is a city renowned for its cultural diversity, and this diversity is beautifully reflected in its cuisine. The city's culinary scene embraces influences from various cultures, including African, Indian, Malay, Chinese, and European, resulting in a vibrant fusion of flavors and techniques. Whether you're a food enthusiast or simply enjoy exploring new tastes, Johannesburg's cuisine offers an array of delightful options.

When navigating Johannesburg cuisine, one of the best tips I can offer is to embrace the local street food culture. Food markets and stalls are scattered throughout the city, showcasing an incredible variety of dishes. Don’t be scared to give them a try.

Alright, so let's start with the iconic Bunny Chow. This is a delicious street food dish that originated in the Indian community of Johannesburg. It consists of a hollowed-out loaf of bread filled with a flavorful curry, often made with chicken, lamb, or beans. This creation is perfect for satisfying your cravings and experiencing the vibrant Indian influence on Johannesburg's culinary scene. It’s hot! Very hot!

Next on our culinary adventure is the beloved boerewors—a traditional South African sausage that holds a special place in Johannesburg's food culture. It is made from a combination of beef, pork, and spices, boerewors is often cooked on the braai (South African barbecue) and served with a side of chakalaka (a spicy vegetable relish) and pap (a maize porridge). The combination of smoky flavors and spicy accompaniments creates a truly memorable dining experience. This is a staple in my own home and many homes in Johannesburg as it is so easy to prepare and put on a bread roll, especially if you are arriving home late from work!

For those seeking a taste of African cuisine, a must-try dish is the hearty and flavorful bobotie. This traditional South African dish is made with spiced minced meat, typically beef or lamb, mixed with dried fruit, herbs, and spices. It's then topped with a layer of savory egg custard and baked The result is a comforting and aromatic dish that showcases the fusion of African and European culinary influences. . All I can say is, you must taste it to believe it!

One dish that cannot be missed is the famous Johannesburg-style barbecue, known as "shisa nyama." Shisa nyama is more than just a meal to most locals. It is a social gathering centered around the art of grilling meat. All you need to do is head to one of the bustling shisa nyama spots where you will find a variety of meats such as beef, chicken, lamb, and boerewors sizzling on open flames. The meat is expertly seasoned and cooked to perfection, resulting in tender and juicy bites bursting with smoky flavors.

Another indigenous dish to try is morogo. This can be described as a traditional African dish featuring dark leafy greens, such as spinach or amaranth, sautéed with onions, tomatoes, and a medley of spices. Morogo is widely known as an extremely nutritious and flavorsome dish that showcases the use of local ingredients. You can eat it together with pap or as a side dish to accompany meat-based meals. Alright, I won't lie, this is one of my least favorites, but still, you should at least try it. Are you really hungry? Then why not try a Kota. This is a unique local take on a sandwich and consists of a hollowed-out quarter loaf of bread filled with various fillings, such as polony (sausage), cheese, eggs, and chutney. It's a hearty and portable snack that's perfect for on-the-go dining.

When navigating Johannesburg's diverse cuisine, it's important to keep an open mind and embrace the flavors and culinary traditions that make this city unique. Don't be afraid to try new dishes and explore the vibrant local food scene. Try to remember that the beauty of exploring the local cuisine provides a opportunity to connect with different cultures, taste new flavors, and create unforgettable culinary memories.

In addition to exploring the vibrant food scene, another tip for navigating Johannesburg cuisine is to engage with the locals. Strike up a conversation with your waiter or fellow diners and ask for recommendations on hidden culinary gems or must-try dishes. There are many locations in Johannesburg that I am yet to explore myself!

18. NOW FOR SOMETHING SWEET

One of my personal favorites. The sweet side of Johannesburg! It’s time for me to help you explore the delectable world of desserts and sweet treats that can be found in this vibrant city. From traditional favorites to modern creations, Johannesburg offers a delightful array of desserts to tempt your taste buds. So, let's dive in and discover some of the must-try sweet treats and where you can find them.

One dessert that you simply must try is malva pudding. This is a sticky and indulgent South African classic as well as a favorite among locals and visitors alike. Malva Pudding is made with apricot jam, butter, sugar, eggs, and a hint of vinegar. This is a moist and rich dessert served warm with a sweet and creamy sauce. The combination of flavors and textures will leave you wanting more. I know I always do! You can find this heavenly treat at many restaurants and cafes throughout Johannesburg but be sure to try it at renowned spots like The Local Grill or Doppio Zero for an exceptional malva pudding experience.

For those like me with a love for chocolate, Johannesburg has you covered. Visit Chocoloza in the suburb of Parkhurst. This is well and truly a chocolate lover's paradise. At Chocoloza you can indulge in handmade artisanal chocolates. From truffles and pralines to chocolate-covered fruits and nuts, Chocoloza offers a wide variety of decadent delights. If I were you, I would make this a day outing and try everything! It's an absolute must-visit for any chocolate enthusiast.

Another one of my personal favorites…ok let's get real…anything sweet is one of my personal favorites, is the Peppermint Crisp Tart. This South African classic dessert consists of layers of crushed biscuits, caramelized condensed milk, whipped cream, and a generous sprinkling of peppermint chocolate. It's a cool and creamy treat that's perfect for a hot Johannesburg day. Look for it on the dessert menus of local restaurants like The Grillhouse or Parea Taverna.

Craving something sweet with a touch of spice? Then you must try koeksisters. These delectable treats take me all the way back to my childhood. They are syrup-drenched, braided pastries made from twisted dough and deep-fried. Once they have been fried, they are soaked in a sweet syrup infused with cinnamon and ginger. You can find them at local bakeries, cafes, and even some supermarkets throughout Johannesburg.

For those who appreciate the simplicity of a classic baked good, a visit to Fournos Bakery is a must. With multiple locations across Johannesburg, Fournos Bakery is a go-to spot for delicious pastries and baked treats. I have tried to make them myself, but nothing tastes the same as it does from Fournos Bakery. Indulge in their selection of freshly baked croissants, Danish pastries, cakes, and cookies.

If you are looking for Paris in Johannesburg, then why not make your way to Patisserie de Paris in the suburb of Greenside. This is a charming French-inspired bakery offering a wide range of mouthwatering desserts, including éclairs, macarons, tarts, and cakes. Their signature raspberry mille-feuille, a delicate pastry filled with layers of cream and tangy raspberry jam will leave you transformed. This bakery is well known for their attention to detail and the exquisite flavors.

Surprisingly, the local markets, such as the Neighbourgoods Market or the Rosebank Sunday Market house a treasure trove of homemade sweets, baked goods, and artisanal treats from local vendors. You will find yourself strolling through the market stalls, sampling an array of confections.

Remember to pace yourself and share these sweet treats with friends or family to truly savor the experience and prevent yourself from getting indigestion! Johannesburg's dessert scene is as diverse as its people, offering something for every sweet craving and preference.

19. JOHANNESBURG RECIPES THAT YOU CAN TAKE HOME WITH YOU

Let's delve into the culinary world of Johannesburg and explore some delicious recipes that tourists can recreate in the comfort of their own homes, no matter where they're from. I'll also provide recommendations for South African cookbooks authored by local chefs, along with tips and guides on ingredient substitutions for those who don't have access to certain ingredients in their home country.

One popular recipe that can be easily recreated is a traditional South African dish called "Bobotie." This fragrant and flavorful dish consists of spiced minced meat, typically beef or lamb, mixed with dried fruit, herbs, and spices. It's then topped with a savory egg-based custard and baked until golden. To make Bobotie at home, tourists can find numerous recipes online or consider purchasing a South African cookbook that features traditional recipes.

Recreating Bunny-Chow at home is a delightful way to experience the fusion of Indian and South African flavors. Prepare a delicious curry of your choice, whether it's chicken, lamb, or vegetarian, and serve it in a hollowed-out bread roll or even a bowl of rice. The combination of spicy curry and bread creates a unique and satisfying meal. A perfect addition to a dinner party with your friends.

So, you have tried Malva Pudding and you would like to recreate it when you get back to your country. are numerous recipes available online that guide you through the process of making this delectable treat. Serve it warm with a scoop of vanilla ice cream for an extra touch of indulgence.

Chakalaka. Probably one of the easiest recipes to recreate. This spicy vegetable relish is a staple in South African cuisine and pairs well with many dishes. It's made with a combination of chopped onions, tomatoes, peppers, carrots, and spices, creating a vibrant and flavorful condiment. Recreate the flavors of Johannesburg by making your own chakalaka at home. You can use it as a side dish to complement grilled meats, as a topping for burgers or sandwiches, or simply enjoy it with some warm bread.

While Milk Tart is not the easiest dessert to make you can certainly give it a try. It is made with a delicate pastry crust filled with a luscious milk and custard-based filling, often flavored with a hint of cinnamon. The combination of the flaky pastry and smooth custard filling will transport you back to the flavors of Johannesburg. All you need is a good cookbook!

No, when it comes to cookbooks, there are several renowned South African authors who have written wonderful recipe collections. One such author is Sarah Graham, known for her book "Bitten: Sarah Graham's Food Safari." In this book, she takes readers on a culinary adventure through South African cuisine, offering a wide range of recipes that showcase the country's diverse culinary heritage. Another author to look out for is Zola Nene, whose cookbook "Simply Delicious" features a collection of easy-to-follow South African recipes that put a modern twist on traditional dishes. I am lucky enough to have both cookbooks tucked away safely in my kitchen drawer.

When recreating these Johannesburg favorites at home, don't be afraid to put your own twist on the recipes. Feel free to adjust the flavors, spices, and ingredients based on your preferences and what's available to you locally. Cooking is an adventure, and adding your personal touch can make the experience even more enjoyable.

It is important to note that when it comes to ingredient substitutions, it's important to be resourceful and creative. If a particular ingredient is not available in your home country, fear not! There are often alternatives that can be used to achieve a similar flavor or texture. For example, if a recipe calls for "biltong," a popular South African dried and cured meat, you can try using beef jerky or another type of dried meat that is easily accessible in your local market. The goal is to find a substitute that provides a similar taste and texture.

Similarly, when it comes to spices and seasonings, you can often find suitable substitutes in your own pantry or local grocery stores. For instance, if a recipe calls for "peri-peri" seasoning, which is a spicy blend of chili peppers, garlic, and other spices, you can use cayenne pepper or a hot sauce with a similar flavor profile. Experiment with different spice combinations and adjust the quantities to achieve the desired level of heat and flavor.

20. HOLIDAY RESORTS

If you are traveling on a budget, there are an array of wonderful holiday self-catering resorts you can find in Johannesburg. These resorts offer a fantastic opportunity to enjoy a comfortable and convenient stay while immersing yourself in the beauty and excitement of Johannesburg.

A good choice is Monateng Safari Lodge. This is a traveler’s haven nestled in a serene setting surrounded by nature's beauty. This establishment offers self-catering chalets providing all the comforts you need. The lodge also offers an array of amenities, including safari drives. And here's a handy tip: Many of these resorts have communal braai (barbecue) areas, so don't forget to grab some local treats like boerewors (South African sausage) and enjoy a traditional South African braai with your fellow guests.

If you're looking for a family-friendly option, look no further than Magalies Park. Many Johannesburg families have spent wonderful holidays at this lovely resort. It is situated in the breathtaking Magaliesberg region and offers self-catering accommodation amidst lush landscapes. There's something for everyone here, from golf and tennis to water sports and leisure activities. Parents can enjoy a round of golf while the kids have a blast at the water park or embark on an exciting canoeing adventure.

For a tranquil escape to the Cradle of Humankind, Glenburn Lodge is the perfect choice. The accommodation here consists of charming self-catering chalets along the picturesque Crocodile River. There are stunning views of rolling hills and access to hiking trails and other recreational activities. You can also spend the day exploring the Cradle of Humankind World Heritage Site which is home to fascinating archaeological discoveries. You should also try to fit in a visit to the Sterkfontein Caves, where ancient fossils have been found, giving insights into human evolution.

And of course, I must mention the renowned Sun City Vacation Club which is just a short drive from

Johannesburg. This is a stunning resort that offers self-catering units and an abundance of activities to keep you entertained all year round. It boasts golf courses, casinos, and water parks so that you'll never have a dull moment. Soak up the sun by the pool, try your luck at the casino, or indulge in a rejuvenating spa treatment. And the food! To die for! The resort boasts a range of dining options that cater to various tastes and preferences. Try local delicacies like sosaties (marinated meat skewers) or samp and beans. And here's a tip: Don't forget to explore the nearby Pilanesberg National Park, a malaria-free wildlife reserve, where you can embark on an unforgettable safari adventure and spot incredible wildlife in their natural habitat.

Now that we've covered some fantastic holiday resorts, let's move on to a few tips to enhance your self-catering experience in South Africa.

When you're staying at a self-catering resort in Johannesburg, it's a great opportunity to try your hand at some easy and delicious local meals. It is important to try and plan your meals in advance. Create a shopping list that includes local ingredients you'd like to try and visit nearby grocery stores or markets to stock up on supplies. This way, you can fully enjoy the flexibility of cooking your own meals and savoring the authentic flavors of South Africa. While self-catering can be a lot of fun try not to limit yourself to just cooking. If you have the means, venture out and explore local restaurants and eateries too.

The resort staff are there to make your experience incredible, so feel free to engage with them. They can provide valuable information about local attractions, activities, or any special events happening during your stay. Their recommendations can help you make the most of your time at the resort and in Johannesburg. Don't hesitate to ask about local customs, traditions, or even suggestions for off-the-beaten-path experiences that will enrich your visit.

21. HIKING AND PICNICS

Get ready to explore the great outdoors and soak up the natural beauty that Johannesburg has to offer. Oh, and don't forget to pack some delicious snacks unique to Johannesburg for a delightful picnic along the way. Here are some tips to make your hiking experience even more enjoyable.

If you're craving a peaceful escape from the city, head to the Klipriviersberg Nature Reserve. This hidden gem offers a serene environment where you can connect with nature. The reserve boasts well-maintained trails that take you through diverse landscapes and introduce you to the local flora and fauna. It's a fantastic opportunity to spot some indigenous wildlife and birdlife. And what's a hiking adventure without some delicious treats? Don't forget to pack some rusks—a South African specialty. These dry biscuits or bread are ideal for nibbling on during your hike. Dip them into a cup of coffee or tea for a true South African experience.

Just a short drive from Johannesburg, you'll find the magnificent Magaliesberg Mountain Range. This picturesque mountain range offers an abundance of hiking trails suitable for all levels of fitness. If I can do it, you can too! Whether you're a leisurely stroller or a seasoned hiker seeking a challenge, there's a trail for you. To keep your energy levels up during your hike, pack some locally sourced dried fruit. Biltong fruit rolls or dried mango slices are perfect choices. They are lightweight, packed with nutrients, and provide a burst of natural sweetness to keep you going.

Another hiking gem near Johannesburg is the Suikerbosrand Nature Reserve. With its vast grasslands and rolling hills, it promises breathtaking vistas and a variety of well-marked trails to explore. Now, for your picnic break, indulge in some traditional South African vetkoek. These deep-fried bread rolls can be filled with savory or sweet fillings of your choice. My personal favorite is chicken mayonnaise, but any filling is divine.

Let's talk about some more Johannesburg-inspired picnic meal ideas that will make your outdoor adventure even more delicious. These meal ideas are perfect to enjoy during your hike and are so easy to eat on the go while you take in the stunning views.

Bobotie Quiches are mini versions of the classic South African dish. These bite-sized quiches are packed with spiced minced meat, raisins, and aromatic spices. The filling is poured into pre-baked tart shells or muffin cups, topped with a whisked egg mixture, and baked until golden and set. Of course, there is no need to make them yourself. You can get them from most bakeries in Johannesburg.

If you're looking for something protein-packed and refreshing, try Biltong Salad Wraps. You can make these with a base of mixed greens, cherry tomatoes, sliced cucumber, and crumbled feta cheese. Next, add strips of biltong—an air-dried, cured meat that's popular in Johannesburg. Drizzle with your favorite dressing, toss it all together, and wrap it in lettuce leaves or whole-grain tortillas. It's a easy to make and flavorful picnic meal that combines the goodness of a salad with a Johannesburg twist!

For the kids, why not go for Vetkoek Sliders? Instead of regular buns, use vetkoek to sandwich your favorite burger fillings—grilled patties, cheese, lettuce, tomato, and your choice of condiments. These mini sliders are a hit among both kids and adults, and they bring a taste of South Africa to your picnic.

Finally, end your picnic on a sweet note with Melktert Parfaits. These individual parfaits layer crushed digestive biscuits or shortbread cookies, creamy custard (like the filling in a traditional melktert), and a sprinkle of cinnamon. You can top them with whipped cream or a dollop of condensed milk if you feel you may need some more sugar during your hike!

When packing your picnic meals, make sure to use containers that are easy to carry and keep everything cool with ice packs or insulated bags. Also, don't forget to bring along some refreshing drinks like homemade rooibos iced tea or locally brewed craft sodas to quench your thirst.

22. GLAMPING VERSUS CAMPING

Let's talk about the awesome camping options in Johannesburg and a unique camping experience called glamping. So, if you're up for some outdoor fun and relaxation, Johannesburg has got you covered. I can say from my own experience that I am not very inclined to opt for camping, but glamping on the other hand is a whole different ballgame!

Glamping is a glamorous twist on traditional camping and combines luxury and comfort with the great outdoors, allowing you to experience nature in style. It's a fantastic option for those who want a unique camping experience without compromising on modern amenities.

In and around Johannesburg, you'll find some incredible glamping opportunities that will elevate your camping experience. Take, for example, Oaklands Country Manor, situated in the picturesque Magaliesberg region. Here, you can stay in luxurious tents equipped with comfortable beds, private bathrooms, and stunning views. You are also able to indulge in gourmet meals prepared by the on-site chef and soak in the peacefulness of nature. It's a wonderful way to enjoy the beauty of Johannesburg's outskirts with a touch of luxury.

Another fantastic glamping option is Buffalo Gorge, located in the Dinokeng Game Reserve. Here, you can experience the thrill of being close to nature while enjoying the comforts of well-appointed tents. Wake up to the sounds of wildlife and embark on game drives, bush walks, and birdwatching activities.

Now, when it comes to traditional camping, you'll find several campgrounds in and around Johannesburg that offer beautiful natural settings and amenities to make your camping experience comfortable. Pitch your own tent and wake up to the sounds of birds chirping and the crisp morning air. Besides having to do it yourself, it's a great way to connect with nature if you are so inclined.

One popular camping spot is the Maropeng Campsite. Located in the Cradle of Humankind World Heritage Site, this campground allows you to camp surrounded by ancient history and stunning landscapes. You can explore nearby attractions like the

Sterkfontein Caves and take in the breathtaking sunsets over the grasslands. And don't forget to bring along your braai (barbecue) essentials for a delicious outdoor cooking experience.

If you're looking for a peaceful camping getaway, consider the Suikerbosrand Nature Reserve. Set up your tent in one of the designated camping areas and get ready to immerse yourself in the tranquility of the wilderness. The reserve offers hiking trails, wildlife sightings, and clear night skies for stargazing. It's the perfect place to unwind and reconnect with nature.

Now, let's talk about meals while camping or glamping in Johannesburg. Keeping it simple and convenient is the name of the game. Here are some ideas for easy and delicious camping meals:

Pack some marinated meats, boerewors (sausages), and kebabs to grill over an open fire. Pair them with fresh salads, roasted veggies, and a side of mieliepap (maize porridge) for a traditional camping feast.

You cannot beat the Potjie. Bring along a cast-iron pot and try making a flavorful potjie. It's a traditional South African dish cooked slowly over hot coals. You can use your choice of meat, vegetables, and spices to create a hearty and comforting meal that will warm your soul.

Or why not keep it simple and delicious with toasted sandwiches. Pack some bread, cheese, and a variety of fillings like ham, tomato, and onion. Use a cast-iron pan or a camping sandwich press to make these tasty treats. They're quick, easy, and perfect for a lunchtime picnic during your camping adventure.

If you have decided to spend time in Johannesburg glamping or camping it is important to check the weather forecast and pack accordingly. Johannesburg can experience temperature fluctuations, so be prepared for both hot and cool conditions. And don't forget your insect repellent and sunscreen to protect yourself from pesky bugs and the sun's rays. Remember to always follow the campground or glamping site's rules and regulations to ensure a respectful and harmonious experience with fellow campers.

23. JOHANNESBURG SAFARIS

Are you ready for an extraordinary journey? The great safari! Let's investigate the world of safari lodges in Johannesburg. A Safari is the perfect way to bring you closer to nature while tantalizing your taste buds with delightful cuisine.

Ivory Tree Game Lodge is nestled within the enchanting Pilanesberg National Park. Here, not only will you be treated to exhilarating wildlife encounters, but you'll also embark on a culinary journey like no other. The lodge's on-site restaurant boasts a menu that showcases a fusion of international and local flavors. From succulent grilled meats prepared on traditional braais to hearty potjie stews simmered to perfection, every bite is a celebration of South African cuisine. Indulge in the rich and aromatic flavors while soaking in the awe-inspiring natural surroundings.

Next up is Madikwe Safari Lodge, a haven of luxury and untamed wilderness. As you unwind after an exciting game drive, you'll find yourself at the lodge's restaurant, where a team of talented chefs awaits to tantalize your taste buds. From traditional

South African delicacies to international culinary delights, the menu caters to a variety of palates. Allow yourself to savor the rich flavors of bobotie or a perfectly grilled fillet steak accompanied by locally sourced vegetables.

Finally, we have Mabula Game Lodge. This is a lodge where luxury accommodations and remarkable wildlife encounters converge. I have had the pleasure of staying at this lodge during a team-building experience and I have to say that it was unforgettable! Here, your taste buds will be treated to a delightful array of flavors. The lodge's restaurant offers a diverse menu that showcases both traditional South African dishes and international favorites. Try the aromatic flavors of a Cape Malay curry, a tantalizing blend of spices and tender meats, or indulge in a perfectly seared ostrich fillet accompanied by indigenous vegetables.

Let's not forget about those game drives and the need for sustenance while exploring the wilderness. Many safari lodges provide snacks for you to enjoy during your adventures. These snacks are carefully selected to provide energy and convenience, allowing you to stay fueled and focused on spotting incredible wildlife. Snack on a mix of dried fruits, nuts, and biltong. These snacks are not only delicious but also easy to pack and enjoy while on the move.

I would like to offer some useful tips to make your safari lodge adventure even more incredible. First and foremost, pack light, but don't forget the essentials. Don't forget your hat, sunscreen, insect repellent, binoculars, and camera to capture those breathtaking moments.

Your safari guides are the experts. Listen attentively to their instructions during game drives, as they know the best spots to spot wildlife and will ensure your safety throughout the adventure. Embrace the magic of night drives. Many safari lodges offer thrilling night game drives. Prepare to be amazed as you venture into the African bush after dark, where you might spot nocturnal creatures in action. It's an experience like no other.

24.THE OFFICIAL LANGUAGES OF JOHANNESBURG

As you navigate through the vibrant streets, you'll encounter a tapestry of languages spoken by different communities, each reflecting their unique heritage. So, let's dive even deeper into this fascinating linguistic journey and discover more about the cultures and cuisines associated with these languages.

English is your trusty companion as you navigate Johannesburg. It serves as the lingua franca, connecting people from various backgrounds and making communication relatively easy for travelers. You'll find that most locals are fluent in English, particularly in tourist areas, hotels, and restaurants. So, don't hesitate to strike up conversations, seek recommendations, or engage in friendly banter with the friendly people you encounter along the way.

Let's explore the rich cultures and delicious cuisines associated with some of the prominent languages in Johannesburg:

isiZulu, one of the most widely spoken languages, carries the vibrant cultural heritage of the Zulu people. The Zulu culture is renowned for its sense of community, vibrant traditional attire, and spirited celebrations. When it comes to cuisine, prepare yourself for a delectable journey. Traditional Zulu dishes are a celebration of flavors and include delights like umngqusho (a hearty dish of samp and beans), amadumbe (a starchy root vegetable often prepared as a side dish or in stews), and mouthwatering grilled meats that are perfectly seasoned and cooked to perfection.

isiXhosa, another prominent language spoken in Johannesburg, is deeply intertwined with the rich Xhosa culture. The Xhosa people are known for their intricate beadwork, colorful traditional clothing, and profound respect for their cultural practices. To truly savor the Xhosa culinary experience, be sure to indulge in dishes like umngqusho (like the Zulu dish but with a unique twist), isophi (a steamed bread that is soft and fluffy), and umleqwa (a free-range chicken dish prepared in various delicious ways).

Afrikaans, a language derived from Dutch, is spoken by the Afrikaans community in Johannesburg. The Afrikaans culture has a fascinating history shaped by European influences, combined with the vibrant spirit of South Africa. When it comes to cuisine, traditional Afrikaans dishes are a true delight. From the iconic bobotie to the flavorful boerewors and the irresistible melktert, each bite tells a story of Afrikaans culinary traditions.

Sepedi, also known as Northern Sotho, is spoken by the Pedi people in Johannesburg. Pedi culture is known for its lively music, vibrant dance, and rich oral traditions. When it comes to cuisine, exploring Sepedi dishes will introduce you to a world of flavors. Savor dikgobe, a hearty sorghum-based porridge served with flavorful stews, mala mogodu, a tender tripe stew cooked to perfection, and morogo, a leafy green vegetable prepared in various ways. These dishes showcase the rich culinary heritage of the Pedi people.

Don't underestimate the power of body language and gestures. A warm smile, a friendly nod, or pointing to something can bridge the language gap and convey your message effectively. Locals will appreciate your effort to connect, even if you don't speak the same language. You will find most Johannesburg locals to be extremely helpful and welcoming.

Immerse yourself in the local culture by attending traditional music and dance performances, visiting local markets, or joining community celebrations. Engage with locals, ask questions, and show genuine interest in their customs. You'll find that people are often eager to share their traditions and create lasting connections.

Bear in mind that Johannesburg is a multicultural city, and while the languages may vary, the warm hospitality and eagerness to connect are universal. So, embrace the diversity, taste the flavors of different cultures, and embark on a linguistic and culinary adventure that will leave you with cherished memories.

25. APPS TO DOWNLOAD BEFORE YOU LEAVE

Before you embark on your exciting journey to Johannesburg, let me fill you in on some essential apps that will make your experience even more convenient and enjoyable. From finding delicious food options to navigating the city with ease, these apps have got you covered. Most Johannesburg residents would be lost without these apps, so grab your smartphone, sit back, and let's dive into the world of digital convenience!

First up, let's talk about transportation. If I didn't have my own vehicle, I would be Ubering everywhere!

Uber is a popular ride-hailing app that operates in Johannesburg. With just a few taps on your phone, you can easily request a ride and explore the city hassle-free. No need to worry about navigating unfamiliar streets or haggling with taxi drivers. Uber will take care of your transportation needs, giving you more time to focus on enjoying your adventure. Plus, it's a reliable and safe option, especially if you're unfamiliar with the local transportation system.

Hungry? Don’t feel like going out? Zomato and Uber Eats are food delivery apps that offer a wide range of restaurant options in Johannesburg. Whether you're craving local South African cuisine, international flavors, or simply need a quick snack, these apps have got you covered. These apps allow you to browse through menus, read reviews, and have your favorite dishes delivered right to your doorstep. It's the perfect solution for those days when you want to relax in your accommodation or have a picnic in a nearby park.

Mr. Delivery is another popular food delivery app that offers a wide range of restaurant options for you to explore. It's a convenient way to satisfy your cravings without leaving the comfort of your accommodation. Simply browse through the app's extensive list of participating restaurants, select your desired dishes, and place your order. From local favorites to international cuisines, Mr. Delivery has something for everyone. You can track your delivery in real-time, ensuring that your meal arrives right on your doorstep. It's a fantastic option for those lazy evenings or when you simply want to enjoy a cozy night in.

These food delivery apps are particularly useful when you want to take a break from exploring the city or have a relaxing evening in your accommodation. They save you time and effort by eliminating the need to search for nearby restaurants or worry about language barriers when ordering over the phone. Plus, you can enjoy your meal at your own pace, whether you prefer dining alfresco on a balcony or cozying up in your hotel room.

Now, let's talk about managing your finances on the go. Consider downloading the banking apps of your respective financial institutions. Nearly every local in Johannesburg has a banking app downloaded onto their phone. These apps provide convenient access to your accounts, allowing you to check balances, make payments, and track transactions. It's a secure and efficient way to stay on top of your financial matters while you explore the vibrant streets of Johannesburg. Whether you need to transfer funds, pay bills, or monitor your spending, these apps ensure that your financial management is just a few taps away.

Remember, it's always a good idea to download these apps before you leave for your trip. This way, you'll have everything ready to go and won't need to worry about Wi-Fi connections or limited data while you're out and about. If you are anything like me, consider organizing them into a dedicated folder on your phone for easy access and to keep everything neatly organized.

26. THE JOHANNESBURG MUSIC AND THEATRE SCENE

From live performances to musical productions and opera, Johannesburg offers a rich tapestry of musical experiences that will leave you captivated. When it comes to musical productions and live performances, Johannesburg has a plethora of venues that cater to diverse tastes.

The Joburg Theatre, located in the heart of the city, is a must-visit destination for theater enthusiasts. It hosts a wide range of shows, including musicals, plays, and dance performances. From captivating Broadway productions to awe-inspiring local talent, the Joburg

Theatre showcases the best of the performing arts scene. As you enjoy the performances, indulge in the delectable cuisine offered at the theater's on-site restaurant or explore nearby eateries for pre-show or post-show meals. The options are endless, ranging from fine dining experiences to cozy cafés that offer a variety of cuisines to suit every palate.

For those seeking classical music experiences, the South African State Theatre is a venue not to be missed. Known for its breathtaking opera productions and classical music concerts, this cultural hub presents a blend of international performances and local talent. Many of these venues offer dining options within the premises, allowing you to indulge in sumptuous meals before or after the show. From elegant restaurants to charming bistros, you can savor a range of cuisines while discussing the intricacies of the performance or simply relishing the magical moments you've experienced.

Another hotspot for music enthusiasts is the Market Theatre, a renowned venue known for its avant-garde productions and diverse music performances. Whether you're interested in jazz, Afrobeat, or contemporary music, the Market Theatre offers a dynamic lineup of shows that cater to various musical tastes. Take a seat in the intimate theaters and let the music transport you to new realms. The venue's on-site restaurant is a perfect spot to enjoy pre-show drinks and a delectable meal. The Market Theatre precinct also houses trendy cafes and bars, where you can engage in lively conversations about the performances and mingle with fellow music lovers.

And now enter the Barnyard Theatre! I don’t want to be biased, but in my opinion, this is the best experience that you can get when it comes to the music scene in Johannesburg! This is a unique and exciting entertainment venue in Johannesburg that combines live music performances with delicious food options. If you are into toe-tapping music, tasty treats, and a whole lot of fun then The Barnyard Theatre is for you!

Its energetic and interactive musical shows cover a wide range of genres and is suitable for the whole family. From rock 'n' roll classics to popular hits and musical tributes, their performances are designed to get you up on your feet and singing along. The talented cast members put on spectacular shows that guarantee a memorable experience for all.

The Barnyard Theatre also offers a variety of delicious dishes that cater to different tastes and preferences. Before the show starts, you can enjoy a meal at their in-house restaurant. The menu features a range of options, from mouthwatering burgers and succulent grilled meats to fresh salads and vegetarian delights. They also have a selection of sides and appetizers to complement your main course.

If you're looking for something lighter, they offer snack platters and finger foods that are perfect for sharing with friends or family. You can munch on crispy chicken wings, loaded nachos, or sliders at your table while enjoying the lively atmosphere of the theatre.

During the show, you'll have the option to order drinks right at your table. Whether you're in the mood for a refreshing cocktail, a glass of wine, or a cold beer, the friendly waitstaff will ensure you're well taken care of throughout the performance. They also offer a variety of snacks, such as popcorn, nuts, and sweet treats, to keep you fueled and satisfied during the show. A firm favorite for many locals and tourists alike.

If you want to navigate the music scene in Johannesburg, a great resource is online event listings and local entertainment publications. Websites such as Computicket and Joburg.co.za provide up-to-date information on upcoming shows, concerts, and musical events. Social media platforms are also a valuable source of information, as many venues and artists promote their events on Facebook, Instagram, and Twitter. Following local musicians, bands, and venues on social media can keep you informed about the latest happenings and ticket sales.

Many musical events sell out quickly, so it's best to book your tickets in advance to secure your spot. Check the ticketing platforms regularly and set reminders for ticket release dates. Also, arriving early not only ensures you get the best seats but also allows you to soak up the atmosphere and explore the venue. You may even have a chance to interact with fellow music enthusiasts or catch a glimpse of the artists before the show.

Lastly, research nearby restaurants or eateries where you can enjoy a pre-show meal or a post-show drink. Many venues have partnerships with local establishments, offering discounts or special packages.

27. ART MUSEUMS

Johannesburg is home to a rich and thriving art scene, with many museums and galleries that showcase a wide range of artistic expressions. One such gem is the Johannesburg Art Gallery, situated in the heart of the city in Joubert Park. This iconic museum houses an extensive collection of artworks, spanning various periods and styles. From classical masterpieces to contemporary works, the gallery provides a glimpse into the diverse artistic heritage of the city. As you stroll through the spacious halls, you'll encounter captivating paintings, thought-provoking sculptures, and mesmerizing ceramics that will transport you to different artistic realms.

"What about food?", you may ask. Many art museums in Johannesburg have on-site cafes or restaurants where you can unwind, refuel, and reflect on the art you've encountered. These establishments often offer a delightful array of cuisine to cater to diverse palates.

A great example is the WAM Cafe at the Wits Art Museum. This is a popular spot for art enthusiasts to grab a bite. Nestled within the museum premises, the cafe offers a menu inspired by local flavors and international influences. You can savor a selection of freshly prepared sandwiches, wraps, and salads, all made with quality ingredients. Pair your meal with a cup of aromatic coffee or indulge in a refreshing beverage.

Another noteworthy destination is the Zeitz Museum of Contemporary Art Africa (MOCAA), situated in the vibrant Silo District. This architectural marvel not only houses a remarkable collection of contemporary artworks but also offers an array of dining options. From casual cafes serving light bites and pastries to elegant restaurants offering innovative gastronomic delights, there's something to satisfy every craving.

Before heading to an art museum, check their opening hours, as they may vary on different days of the week. It's also a good idea to research any ongoing exhibitions or special events to make the most of your visit. Some museums offer discounted or free entry on specific days or for certain age groups, so keep an eye out for such opportunities.

Art museums are meant to be savored, so allow yourself ample time to wander through the galleries. Take a leisurely stroll, pause in front of artworks that captivate you, and let them evoke emotions and spark inspiration. Read the accompanying descriptions or listen to audio guides to gain deeper insights into the artworks and the artists behind them.

Art museums have guidelines in place to preserve the integrity of the artworks and ensure a pleasant experience for all visitors. Respect any photography restrictions, maintain a respectful distance from the artworks, and refrain from touching them unless specifically permitted. By adhering to these rules, you contribute to the preservation of these invaluable cultural treasures.

When visiting art museums in Johannesburg, remember that each museum has its own distinct atmosphere and offerings. Some may have additional facilities, such as bookshops or gift stores, where you can browse and purchase art-related publications, prints, or souvenirs. Take advantage of these resources to extend your art appreciation beyond the museum walls.

28. SPORTS AND RECREATION

Now I don't quite know why anybody travelling overseas would want to go to the gym, but I respect the fact that there are millions of people in the world that do. If you are a fitness enthusiast lets dive into the world of sports, gyms, and recreational fitness facilities in Johannesburg.

Johannesburg offers a range of sports facilities and fitness centers to cater to different interests and fitness levels. One popular spot is Virgin Active, a well-known gym chain with branches throughout the city. They provide a wide range of workout equipment, including cardio machines, weightlifting stations, and group fitness classes. You can push your limits in a high-intensity training session or find your Zen in a calming yoga class. After a rewarding workout, head to their on-site health cafes, where you can refuel with delicious and nutritious options like protein-packed salads, smoothies, and freshly squeezed juices.

For those seeking a more holistic fitness experience, Yoga Works Studio is a must-visit. Yes, I have been here! This serene studio offers a variety of yoga classes suitable for all levels, from beginners to advanced practitioners. With its peaceful ambiance and experienced instructors, you can find inner balance while working on strength, flexibility, and mindfulness. After a rejuvenating yoga session, you can treat yourself to a nutritious post-workout meal at one of the nearby health-conscious cafes, such as Leafy Greens or The Fussy Vegan, where you'll find a range of plant-based delights to nourish your body.

Look for fitness centers or sports facilities near your accommodation or in the areas you plan to visit. Popular gym chains like Planet Fitness, Fit24, and CrossFit boxes are scattered throughout the city and offer a range of fitness options to suit your preferences.

Bring comfortable workout clothes, athletic shoes, and any other necessary gear for your preferred activities. Also, consider packing a reusable water bottle to stay hydrated during your workouts. You can also explore local markets and health food stores for fresh produce and nutritious snacks to keep you energized and nourished throughout the day.

Johannesburg offers unique fitness classes that embrace local culture and traditions. Consider trying a class like Zumba with a South African twist or learning traditional African dance moves to add an extra flair to your workout routine.

29. SPECIAL OCCASIONS

A special occasion in Johannesburg is the perfect excuse to celebrate in style! Whether you're marking a milestone, a romantic evening, or simply want to indulge in a memorable experience, this vibrant city has plenty of options to make your special occasion truly unforgettable. Let me be your guide and show you some fantastic places that I personally know of where you can create cherished memories.

For a romantic night out, you can't go wrong with a visit to Marble Restaurant. This elegant establishment is the very same establishment where my husband proposed to me. It is nestled in the trendy Keyes Art Mile precinct, offers a unique dining experience. Marble is renowned for its sophisticated ambiance, stunning decor, and panoramic views of the city.

The menu at the Marble Restaurant features a fusion of South African and international flavors. From steaks grilled to perfection to fresh seafood prepared with finesse, every bite at Marble is a culinary delight. Pair your meal with a carefully selected South African wine from their extensive wine list and allow the attentive staff to guide you through the culinary journey. The combination of tasty cuisine, stunning views, and impeccable service makes The Marble the perfect choice for a romantic celebration.

Another exquisite venue for special occasions is DW Eleven-13, a fine dining restaurant located in the leafy suburb of Dunkeld West. This is an award-winning establishment and a haven for food enthusiasts seeking a culinary adventure. As you enter DW Eleven-13, you'll be greeted by an inviting atmosphere that exudes elegance and sophistication. The restaurant's attention to detail is evident in both its decor and its carefully curated menu.

The chef's innovative approach to contemporary cuisine ensures that each dish is a work of art. From beautifully plated tasting menus to creative flavor combinations, DW Eleven-13 takes you on a gastronomic journey that will leave you craving for more. The culinary experience is complemented by an extensive wine list, featuring both local and international selections.

If you're looking for a unique dining experience combined with cultural immersion, consider visiting Maboneng Precinct. This vibrant neighborhood is known for its artistic flair and eclectic mix of restaurants and cafes. Here, you can choose from a variety of cuisines, ranging from African fusion to international delights. Enjoy a leisurely dinner at a rooftop restaurant while gazing at the city lights, or savor street food at a bustling market. From traditional African dishes to global gastronomic fusions, Maboneng Precinct offers an array of choices to suit every palate and preference.

To secure your spot at the restaurant of your choice, it's advisable to make reservations well in advance, especially for popular venues. This ensures that you have a guaranteed table on your special day and avoids any disappointment. Many restaurants offer special packages or menus designed specifically for celebrations. These packages may include extras like customized menus, complimentary drinks, or even a personalized cake. Inquire about these options when making your reservation to make your occasion even more memorable and tailored to your preferences.

Take the opportunity to dress up for your special occasion. Most fine dining establishments have dress codes, so make sure to check the requirements before you go. Dressing up not only adds to the ambiance but also enhances your overall experience, making you feel more immersed in the celebration that is Johannesburg!

30. THE HISTORY OF JOHANNESBURG'S FAVORITE FOODS

Let's dive into the fascinating history of Johannesburg's delicious foods and uncover the flavors that define this incredible city. Get ready to tantalize your taste buds and discover some more mouthwatering dishes that are a must-try on your culinary adventure.

A popular and delicious dish in Johannesburg is "Potjiekos." This traditional South African stew is cooked in a three-legged cast-iron pot called a "potjie." The potjie is filled with layers of meat, vegetables, and aromatic spices, creating a rich and flavorful one-pot meal. Potjiekos is more than just a dish; it's a social gathering and a celebration of community. It's a common sight to see friends and family gathered around the potjie, sharing stories, and enjoying the slow-cooked goodness. The dish has its roots in the Dutch settlers and their cooking traditions, which were influenced by the flavors and ingredients of the indigenous people. You can often find Potjiekos being enjoyed at traditional South African restaurants or even at organized outdoor events and festivals.

If you're a fan of seafood, then "Snoek Braai" is a must-try when in Johannesburg. Snoek is a type of fish found in the coastal waters of South Africa, and it is particularly famous for its delicious and delicate flavor. A Snoek Braai involves grilling the fish over an open flame, to create a smoky and slightly charred taste. It's often basted with a marinade made from apricot jam, lemon juice, and a touch of spices, enhancing the natural flavors of the fish. This classic South African dish is a favorite among locals, and it perfectly captures the coastal essence in the heart of Johannesburg.

Johannesburg's street food scene is as different as they come! From flavorful samoosas (fried pastry filled with savory fillings) to boerewors rolls (sausage rolls), exploring the local street food is a must. Seek out food markets, food trucks, and popular street food vendors to savor these tasty and convenient treats.

Try to find eateries specializing in Ethiopian, Nigerian, or Moroccan cuisine, where you can sample dishes like injera (fermented flatbread), jollof rice, or tagines. These restaurants provide a culinary journey through the different regions of Africa, allowing you to experience a variety of unique flavors.

Keep an eye out for food festivals and events happening in Johannesburg. These gatherings celebrate the city's culinary culture, bringing together a diverse range of food vendors, live music, and entertainment. It's a fantastic opportunity to sample a wide array of dishes, interact with local chefs, and soak up the vibrant atmosphere.

Johannesburg's food scene is known for its fusion of flavors and culinary innovation. Look for restaurants that combine different culinary traditions, such as African-European fusion or Afro-Asian fusion. These establishments often offer unique and exciting combinations of ingredients, resulting in a truly unforgettable dining experience.

31. SWEETS AND TREATS

If you have a craving for all things sweet and chocolatey, Johannesburg is the place to be. Get ready to indulge in a delightful adventure as we explore some of the city's sweet and chocolate shops, as well as a few factories that will satisfy your sweet cravings and provide a behind-the-scenes look at the confectionery-making process.

In the trendy suburb of Maboneng, you'll find "Chocoloza," an artisanal chocolate boutique. Situated in the vibrant Arts on Main precinct, this delightful shop offers a range of handcrafted chocolates made with ethically sourced African cocoa beans. Indulge in their signature bonbons, truffles, and chocolate bars, beautifully crafted and bursting with flavor. You won't regret this one!

For a taste of Johannesburg's unique confectionery, head to "The Counter" in the vibrant neighborhood of Braamfontein. This sweet shop specializes in nostalgic treats and old-fashioned candies that will transport you back in time. Explore their selection of handmade nougat, toffees, and rock candies that will delight your taste buds.

In the leafy suburb of Sandton, you'll find "Dolci Café," a cozy café that serves delicious meals and a range of mouthwatering chocolate creations. Take the time to indulge in their selection of chocolate cakes, tarts, and brownies, all made with love and meticulous attention to detail. Don't forget to try one of my all-time favorites, their decadent hot chocolate for a truly memorable experience.

For an interesting experience in nougat-making, visit the "Nougat Factory" in the suburbs of Krugersdorp. Take a guided tour and learn about the art of nougat production, from mixing the ingredients to cutting and packaging. Discover the history of nougat-making and enjoy tastings of their delectable creations.

Johannesburg is also home to a few sweet factories where you can witness the confectionery-making process up close. Here are a couple of notable sweet factories in Johannesburg:

"Ma Mere Confections" in Randburg is a family-owned sweet factory that specializes in handcrafted fudge and toffee creations. Using traditional recipes and techniques, they produce a wide range of fudges in various flavors, from classic chocolate and vanilla to unique combinations like salted caramel and coffee. Take a factory tour to see how these treats are made, from the careful boiling of ingredients to the wrapping and packaging process.

"The Candy Factory" in Germiston is in the eastern part of Johannesburg, The Candy Factory is a haven for candy lovers. This factory produces a wide array of hard candies, gummies, and other sweet treats. Take a guided tour to witness the production process, including mixing and molding the candy, and learn about the intricate art of candy-making. At the end of the tour, go for a tasting session where you can sample a variety of candies made right on-site. The kids will love this one!

Visiting these sweet factories allows you to not only experience the end products but also gain insight into the craftsmanship and dedication that goes into creating these treats. It's a chance to see firsthand how the confectioners work their magic and to appreciate the artistry behind the sweet creations.

Many sweet shops or factories offer guided tours that provide insights into the confectionery-making process. These tours give you a chance to learn about the ingredients, techniques, and stories behind the sweets. They also offer a unique behind-the-scenes look and are often accompanied by delightful tastings.

These visits provide a unique behind-the-scenes experience and an opportunity to learn more about the sweet-making process in Johannesburg. But remember to check the websites or contact the factories in advance to inquire about tour availability and any specific requirements.

Johannesburg is home to many talented confectioners and chocolatiers who pour their passion into creating exceptional treats. Take the opportunity to support local businesses and taste the handcrafted flavors that make Johannesburg's sweet scene so special.

32. THE BEST BAKERIES

I think it is time to embark on a journey through Johannesburg's best bakeries. Whether you're a fan of flaky pastries, artisan bread, or cakes, this city has a bakery for you! Let's explore some of the top bakeries you should visit during your time in Johannesburg.

One bakery that should be at the top of your list is "Patisserie de Paris" in Sandton. This French bakery offers an array of pastries and baked goods that will transport you to the streets of Paris. Indulge in their buttery croissants and delicate macarons. Make sure to try their heavenly éclairs! The bakery also serves a variety of French-style bread and amazing cakes.

If you are looking for artisanal bread and pastries, head over to "Bread & Co" in Parkhurst. This bakery takes pride in crafting its bread using traditional techniques and high-quality ingredients. From crusty sourdough loaves to fluffy brioche, Bread & Co offers a wide selection of bread that will have you coming back for more. Be sure to try their pastries like their flaky croissants, Danishes, and savory quiches. This bakery is situated in a trendy neighborhood and is the perfect spot to enjoy a freshly baked treat along with a good cup of coffee.

If you are a cake lover like me then "The Velvet Cake Co" in Edenvale is a must-visit. This bakery is renowned for its show-stopping cakes that not only taste incredible but also look like edible works of art. The Velvet Cake Co offers a wide range of flavors and designs to suit every occasion. Treat yourself to a slice of their famous red velvet cake or try one of their decadent chocolate creations. If you are really feeling naughty, then try both!

If you are looking for more traditional baked goods, take a trip to "Cosy Corner Bakery" in Melville. This bakery specializes in iconic local treats like "Melktert" (milk tart) and "Hertzoggies" (sweet pastry filled with apricot jam and coconut). These pastries are deeply rooted in South African culinary heritage, and Cosy Corner Bakery serves them up with love and authenticity. Grab a seat in their cozy café and enjoy the nostalgic flavors of these beloved classics.

If you find yourself in the vibrant suburb of Maboneng, don't miss "The Artisan Bakery." This bakery prides itself on using organic and locally sourced ingredients to create a range of bread, pastries, and cakes. From rustic sourdough loaves to delectable fruit tarts, their offerings are made with care and attention to detail. The Artisan Bakery also has a café where you can savor their baked goods alongside a cup of freshly brewed coffee. Remember to buy some goods to take back with you to your accommodation.

Many bakeries in Johannesburg have a loyal following, and their popular items tend to sell out quickly. To ensure you get your hands on the freshest and most sought-after treats, try to visit the bakeries early in the day when the selection is at its best.

Don't be shy to ask the friendly staff for their personal recommendations. They're usually happy to guide you toward their specialty items or popular favorites. It's a great way to discover new flavors and hidden gems within the bakery's offerings.

If you can't resist the temptation of trying everything in one sitting (and who can blame you?), consider getting some treats to take away. Johannesburg's bakeries often offer beautifully packaged goodies that make perfect souvenirs or gifts for the rest of the family.

33. THE NIGHT LIFE IN JOHANNESBURG

When the sun sets in Johannesburg, the city comes alive with an infectious energy. Both young and old travelers are spoilt for choice with an array of trendy bars and lounges to lively nightclubs and live music venues. So, if you're a tourist looking to experience the true essence of Johannesburg after dark, get ready for an unforgettable night out.

One place that must be on your list is the lively Maboneng Precinct. Having visited Maboneng Precinct many times before I can assure you that it offers a fantastic mix of bars, clubs, and restaurants. If you're a fan of live music and jazz, you'll love "The Marabi Club”. This is where talented musicians take the stage and captivate the audience with soulful tunes. To add to the experience why not sip on a cocktail and immerse yourself in the electric atmosphere. And for the hungry, Maboneng has many choices from local South African dishes to exotic international cuisines.

If you are looking for the bohemian side of Johannesburg, head over to the suburb of Melville. This eclectic neighborhood is known for its cafes, bars, and live music venues. Start your evening at "Hell's Kitchen," a local favorite, where you can unwind with a refreshing drink and treat yourself to some scrumptious pub-style food. As the night progresses, be sure to make your way to "Ratz Bar," where the party really gets started! The live music and a buzzing dance floor will make you dance until the early hours.

Rosebank is another neighborhood that offers a fantastic nightlife experience. If you're a music lover, you won't want to miss "Park House of Events on 7." This vibrant venue hosts an array of live performances and showcases talented local and international artists across various genres. As a bonus, Rosebank also has a variety of restaurants that serve dishes from around the world. Whether you're in the mood for Asian fusion, Mediterranean delights, or traditional South African flavors, you'll find it here.

If you are looking for a truly unique and culturally rich experience, consider making your way to Soweto. Vilakazi Street is the heart and soul of Soweto and home to lively bars and restaurants where you can enjoy the vibrant atmosphere. Dig into some mouthwatering braai (barbecue), accompanied by pap (maize porridge) and chakalaka (spicy relish). While you're in Soweto, be sure not to miss the "Soweto Theatre" where you can watch captivating live performances, from music to theater and comedy shows. What a wonderful way to immerse yourself in the local arts and culture scene!

Or, if you're in the mood for a more upscale and cosmopolitan night out, Sandton is the place to be. Sandton is well known for its luxurious bars, lounges, and nightclubs. "Alice & Fifth," an elegant venue that oozes sophistication. They also serve Mediterranean and South African fusion cuisine, so take your pick. If you're in the mood to dance the night away, head to "Movida," a trendy nightclub that hosts top-notch

South African DJs spinning the latest beats. This is where I had my bachelorette party, and it did not disappoint!

Like in any big city, it's important to stay aware of your surroundings and take necessary precautions. Stick to well-lit areas, and travel with a group if possible. Also, try and avoid displaying expensive belongings.

Johannesburg is a sprawling city, so it's a good idea to plan your transportation ahead of time. Consider using reliable ride-sharing services like Uber or arrange for a designated driver if you're driving, especially if you have been consuming alcohol, which no doubt you will if you are looking to dance the night away!

It is important, before heading out, to check online listings or local event calendars to see if there are any special events or performances happening during your visit. This way, you can make the most of your night and catch some incredible live music or entertainment.

34. ADVENTURE IS EVERYWHERE

Johannesburg offers an abundance of adrenaline-pumping activities that will have your heart racing and your spirit soaring. From bungee jumping and paragliding to white river rafting, the adventure possibilities are endless.

One of the must-visit destinations for thrill-seekers is the "Orlando Towers" in Soweto. These towering structures were once part of a decommissioned power station but have now been transformed into an adrenaline playground. If you want an adrenalin rush you can bungee jump from the top of the towers and afterward, satisfy your hunger with some traditional South African cuisine. While bungee jumping is not for all of us, me included, you will still have a good time watching people daringly jump off the towers. There are food stalls nearby where you can try out the tasty local dishes.

If paragliding is on your bucket list, then be sure to head to the beautiful "Magaliesberg" mountain range, located just outside of Johannesburg. The experienced paragliding instructors will guide you through the process, ensuring a safe and exhilarating flight. After your flight, treat yourself to a well-deserved meal at one of the local restaurants. Many of them offer a fusion of flavors, blending South African dishes with international influences.

For a thrilling water adventure, make your way to the "Vaal River" for some white river rafting. They have expert guides that are there to ensure your safety while providing you with an unforgettable experience. After your river escapade you can enjoy a meal by the riverside. Some venues offer a variety of cuisine options, from hearty South African barbecue (braai) to international dishes. Relax, enjoy the scenic surroundings, and savor the flavors of a well-deserved meal.

If you're craving even more excitement, head to "Wild Cave Adventures" in the Cradle of Humankind World Heritage Site. Here, you can explore the mysterious underground world of caves and tunnels. Follow experienced guides as you squeeze through narrow passages, crawl through tunnels, and marvel at the fascinating rock formations. It's an adventure that will leave you in awe of nature's wonders. After emerging from the depths of the caves, replenish your energy at a nearby restaurant. Many establishments in the Cradle of Humankind serve up delectable dishes inspired by local ingredients, giving you a taste of the region's culinary delights.

If you're a fan of zip-lining and aerial adventures, you must head to the "Acrobranch Adventure Park" in Melrose. This treetop venue offers an array of thrilling zip lines, suspension bridges, and Tarzan swings. The park provides a variety of courses suitable for all ages and skill levels, making it a perfect adventure for families with children. After conquering, or watching, your loved ones conquer the tree canopies, refuel at the park's cafe, which offers light meals, snacks, and refreshing beverages.

It is always advisable to prioritize your safety by choosing reputable adventure providers and ensuring they adhere to safety regulations. Listen attentively to the instructions provided by the guides and don't hesitate to ask any questions or voice any concerns you may have.

Some adventure activities may have age or health restrictions, so it's important to check these requirements beforehand. Ensure that you meet the necessary criteria to participate in the activities you're interested in before you make your way to the venue.

As I have mentioned before, Johannesburg's weather can be unpredictable, so be prepared for changing conditions. Dress in layers, carry sunscreen and bring rain gear if necessary. Always pack some extra water and snacks to keep yourself hydrated and energized throughout the day.

35. HOW TO EAT

In Johannesburg, you'll find a mix of eating styles, from eating with your hands to using knives and forks. This, of course, depends on the dish and the dining experience.

When it comes to the traditional braai, eating with your hands is the way to go. The locals often use their fingers to grab a piece of meat and savor the smoky flavors. It's all about the primal joy of indulging in tender, flame-kissed goodness. So, be prepared to get your hands a little messy and enjoy the true essence of a South African braai experience. Keep in mind that anything goes, so if you prefer to use cutlery do so by all means!

Now, let's switch gears to a more refined dining setting. In many Johannesburg restaurants, you'll find that locals often use knives and forks for their meals. This is particularly true when enjoying dishes like bobotie. At these establishments, it is customary to use your utensils to savor the flavorful layers and enjoy the combination of flavors.

When it comes to traditional South African stews like potjiekos or bredie, you'll find locals using knives and forks. I personally prefer to use a tablespoon! These slow-cooked dishes, often prepared in a cast-iron pot, feature tender meats, hearty vegetables, and aromatic spices. Of course, you can use your hands, but this may become a bit messy!

Some dishes offer a flexible dining experience, where you can choose to eat them with your hands or opt for cutlery. For example, when it comes to enjoying Bunny Chow, it's common to eat it with your hands. The bread serves as a delicious vessel to scoop up every bit of the flavorful curry. However, if you prefer, you can also use a knife and fork to enjoy this delectable dish.

When it comes to street food like boerewors rolls or Gatsby sandwiches, the locals often eat them with their hands. These are perfect for a quick, on-the-go snack. Eating these street foods with your hands allows you to fully appreciate the burst of flavors and textures in each bite.

Don't be afraid to dive into the local customs and dining traditions. Trying different eating styles adds to the authenticity of your culinary adventure. Pay attention to how the locals around you enjoy their meals. If you're unsure about whether to eat a specific dish with your hands or cutlery, follow their lead.

Most importantly, whichever eating style you choose, remember to savor the flavors, spices, and textures of Johannesburg's diverse cuisine. Let your taste buds dance and immerse yourself in the culinary delights of the city.

36. FOR THOSE WHO WANT A VIEW

There is nothing better than eating your lunch or dinner while gazing at a spectacular view. Lucky for you, Johannesburg has some incredible dining establishments that not only offer delectable cuisine but also provide breathtaking vistas to enhance your dining experience.

If a view is what you desire, then look no further than the "Living Room" in Maboneng. This rooftop eatery offers a laid-back atmosphere with panoramic views of the city skyline. This restaurant is known for its vibrant cocktails and a variety of tapas-style dishes. Ideal for sharing and sampling different flavors from sliders to zesty ceviche, there's something for everyone to enjoy.

If you're looking for a dining experience amidst nature's splendor, head to "Casalinga" in Muldersdrift. With sprawling grounds and beautiful gardens, this restaurant offers a serene and picturesque setting. You can enjoy your meal al fresco, surrounded by lush greenery and tranquil ponds. "Casalinga" specializes in

Italian cuisine, serving up authentic Italian dishes. Try their homemade pasta, wood-fired pizzas, and classic Italian desserts. They also have an extensive wine list featuring local and international selections, making it the perfect spot for wine enthusiasts.

For a unique dining experience with stunning wildlife views, visit "Moyo Zoo Lake" in Parkview. This restaurant sits on the edge of a picturesque lake, offering scenic views and the opportunity to spot various bird species. The setting is enchanting, with vibrant African-inspired decor and live entertainment that adds to the festive atmosphere. "Moyo" serves up a fusion of African cuisine, showcasing flavors and dishes from different regions of the continent. Their signature dishes are bobotie spring rolls or slow-cooked lamb shank. You can chase your meal down with a refreshing African-inspired cocktails.

These popular spots can fill up quickly, especially during peak times or on weekends so it would be advisable to make a reservation in advance to secure your table and ensure a seamless dining experience. Consider visiting during sunset or the early evening hours to witness the magical transformation of Johannesburg's skyline as the city lights come alive.

Always remember that while some of these restaurants have a stylish ambiance, it's still important to dress comfortably. Also, bear in mind that some venues have specific dress codes, so it's a good idea to inquire beforehand.

37. CURRY IN A HURRY

If you're craving the aromatic flavors of Indian cuisine while exploring Johannesburg, you're in for a treat. This vibrant city is home to several establishments that serve delicious Indian dishes, transporting your taste buds to the streets of Mumbai or the bustling markets of Delhi!

One extremely popular Indian restaurant in Johannesburg is "The Raj" located in Sandton. This is an upscale establishment that offers a refined dining experience with a wide array of Indian dishes on its menu. They have a variety of meals to choose from such as biryanis and creamy butter chicken to vegetarian options like paneer tikka masala. The Raj is well-known for using high-quality ingredients and traditional cooking techniques to create authentic

Indian dishes. The restaurant's elegant ambiance and attentive service also add to your dining experience.

If you feel like a more casual setting with a modern twist, you should head to "Saffron Indian Kitchen" in Rivonia. This eatery combines traditional Indian flavors with an amazing presentation. Their menu features a fusion of Indian and global cuisine, and their menu offers dishes such as tandoori lamb chops, chicken tikka tacos, and naan flatbreads stuffed with a variety of fillings. Saffron Indian Kitchen places a strong emphasis on fresh ingredients and vibrant flavors, creating a unique dining experience that showcases the diversity of Indian cuisine.

For an authentic taste of South Indian flavors, visit "Dosa Hut" in Fordsburg. This restaurant specializes a South Indian dish, the dosa. The dosa is a thin, crispy pancake made from fermented rice and lentil batter, served with a variety of savory fillings and chutneys. At Dosa Hut, you can choose from an extensive range of dosas, including classic options like masala dosa (filled with spiced potatoes) or a little more adventurous creations like paneer tikka dosa (filled with marinated cottage cheese). The restaurant's laid-back atmosphere and affordable prices make it a popular spot among locals and tourists alike.

If you're accustomed to Indian food from other parts of the world, you may find that the "mild" and "hot" levels in Johannesburg are a little different. South African Indian cuisine tends to have a spicier profile compared to some other regions. So, when ordering, it's important to communicate your preferred spice level clearly to ensure a pleasant dining experience.

If you're unsure about what to order or want to try something new, don't hesitate to ask the restaurant staff for their recommendations. They are knowledgeable about the menu and can guide you toward popular and authentic dishes. Indian cuisine is known for its vibrant flavors and variety of dishes so you should consider sharing multiple dishes with your fellow diners to sample a range of flavors and textures.

Indian cuisine often comes with an array of accompaniments like naan bread, papadums, and various chutneys. These side dishes complement the main course and enhance the overall dining experience. Don't forget to try them alongside your chosen dishes. Save some space, however, for dessert.

Indian desserts are a sweet treat that you don't want to miss. From the rich and creamy kulfi (Indian ice cream) to the syrup soaked Gulab jamun (deep-fried milk dumplings), there's a dessert for everyone!

38. FOR THE MEAT LOVER

Calling all meat lovers! If you're in Johannesburg and find yourself yearning for an extraordinarily meaty experience, you're in luck. Johannesburg is home to many remarkable restaurants that cater specifically to meat lovers, So, let's explore some outstanding establishments that will satiate your carnivorous cravings.

First up we have the "Carnivore," which is an absolute paradise for meat lovers. Located in Muldersdrift, when you step into this restaurant, you'll be greeted by the aromas of sizzling meat mixed with the sounds of nature. Situated on a game reserve, Carnivore offers an experience like no other. Their menu includes kudu, impala, and ostrich. What is nice about this restaurant is that they are continuously serving you as the waiters roam around with skewers of perfectly grilled meat, carving portions directly onto your plate. The rustic ambiance, combined with the thrill of indulging in exotic game meats, makes this a meat lover's dream.

“The Local Grill" nestled in Parktown North is renowned for its commitment to sourcing the finest, locally reared meats for your enjoyment. Here you can sink your teeth into perfectly aged beef cuts, tender and succulent lamb chops, and expertly grilled pork ribs. The Local Grill's warm and inviting atmosphere sets the stage for a memorable dining experience, where you can truly appreciate the craftsmanship of a perfectly cooked steak.

If you're seeking a trendy dining destination with a focus on meat, look no further than "The Butcher Shop and Grill" in Sandton. This upscale steakhouse prides itself on serving the finest cuts of meat, sourced from top-quality suppliers. From perfectly aged steaks to grilled lamb chops and hearty beef burgers, the menu is a meat lover's paradise. The Butcher Shop and Grill also offers a variety of sauces and sides to accompany your meaty feast, allowing you to customize your dining experience. Coupled with the sophisticated ambiance and attentive service this restaurant is the perfect place to make meaty memories!

One of the best meat lover's restaurants in Johannesburg, in my opinion, is "Rodizio Brazilian Grill" in Fourways. This lively restaurant offers a unique dining experience centered around a traditional Brazilian concept. Here, the waiters, known as "passadores," parade around the dining area with skewers of succulent, fire-roasted meats, serving you generous portions right at your table. You can feast on tender beef, chicken, and juicy pork, all expertly prepared and bursting with mouthwatering flavors. The energetic vibe, accompanied by lively music and entertaining samba-inspired performances simply adds to the overall experience.

Johannesburg is known for its unique flavors and culinary traditions so if you love meat then you should not miss the chance to try South African meat specialties when you visit. If you are not sure what to choose then why not share meals with the friends or family who are with you. This way, you can enjoy a diverse range of meats and explore different cuts and flavors together and then go back again for more!

It is always a good idea to combine your experience with a selection of local South African craft beers or wines. Johannesburg has an out of this world craft beer scene, and many restaurants offer an impressive array of locally produced beverages that beautifully complement the flavors of the meats.

39. FOR THE VEGETARIAN AND VEGAN

If you're searching for vegetarian and vegan-friendly options in Johannesburg, there are several options to choose from. From innovative creations to traditional favorites, there's something for every veggie lover in this city.

I will start with "Leafy Greens Café" in Muldersdrift. They're all about farm-to-table goodness, using fresh organic ingredients to whip up nourishing dishes. If you are in the mood for a tasty salad bursting with color, hearty grain bowls packed with goodness, or a plant-based burgers that'll make your mouth water then this café is well worth the trip. The best part? The guilt-free desserts and freshly squeezed juices! With its serene ambiance and focus on natural, nutritious cuisine, Leafy Greens Café is a must-visit for all plant-based foodies.

Looking for comfort food with a vegan twist? "Lexi's Healthy Eatery" in Sandton is the place to go. This trendy joint takes vegan dining to new heights and offers a menu that showcases the incredible versatility and deliciousness of plant-based cuisine. You'll find loaded vegan burgers, scrumptious vegan pizzas, and colorful Buddha bowls that are as beautiful as they are nutritious.

If you're craving authentic Indian flavors, you must try "The Great Eastern Food Bar" in Melville. This eatery brings together the vibrant spices of Indian cuisine with vegetarian and vegan-friendly twist. Choose from aromatic curries, flavorful biryanis, and spiced dishes like chana masala (spiced chickpea curry), palak paneer (spinach and cottage cheese), and baingan bharta (smoky roasted eggplant curry). The Great Eastern Food Bar offers a wonderful fusion of traditional Indian flavors and contemporary plant-based dining, in an extremely warm and welcoming setting.

Craving fresh and wholesome vegan fare? "Conscious 108" in Greenside has got you covered. This health-conscious restaurant is all about nourishing your body with plant-based goodness. They use locally sourced, organic ingredients to create dishes that are as delicious as they are nutritious. From chickpea wraps to tofu stir-fries and raw vegan desserts, Conscious 108 offers a holistic dining experience that'll leave you feeling satisfied and well…healthy and energized.

Johannesburg's vegetarian and vegan restaurants are culinary playgrounds where flavors come alive. Don't be afraid to explore new tastes and experiment with different dishes. You'll be amazed at the incredible variety and creativity of plant-based cuisine. I must say that even though I am a meat eater, I have been to some of these establishments, and the experience was well worth it. While many restaurants in Johannesburg are veggie-friendly, it's always a good idea to communicate your dietary preferences to the staff.

40. FUSSY EATERS

So. if you're planning a trip to Johannesburg with your little ones, they are in for a treat! Johannesburg offers a variety of kid-friendly restaurants that go the extra mile to ensure a memorable dining experience for the whole family. From delicious food to engaging activities, these establishments have something for everyone.

One restaurant that should be on your radar is "Happily Ever Laughter" in Sandton. This whimsical eatery combines delicious cuisine with a delightful entertainment experience for kids. Let the kids enjoy interactive storytelling sessions, puppet shows, face painting and crafts. This restaurant knows how to keep young ones entertained while you enjoy a tasty meal. The menu offers a range of family-friendly options, from kid-sized portions of classic favorites like burgers and pizzas to healthier choices like grilled chicken and vegetable wraps. Certainly, a win-win for everyone in the family.

If you're looking for a place where kids can unleash their creativity while enjoying a delicious meal, head to "Play Town" in Fourways. This unique restaurant combines a dining area with a supervised indoor play zone, ensuring that kids have a blast while you enjoy your meal knowing that your little one is in safe hands. The play zone is equipped with slides, ball pits, and interactive play structures, providing endless entertainment for children of all ages. The menu features a variety of dishes that cater to both kids and adults, from hearty burgers and fries to fresh salads and sandwiches.

If you're seeking a relaxing and picturesque setting where your older kids can roam free and explore while you dine, check out "Delta Café" in Craighall Park. Here you will find a spacious outdoor seating area surrounded by lush greenery with a dedicated play area with swings, jungle gyms, and a sandpit. Enjoy your meal and unwind while the kids are kept busy. The menu has a range of options, from hearty breakfasts and gourmet sandwiches to tasty desserts and freshly brewed coffee.

For a fun-filled dining adventure that combines great food with entertainment for kids, "Panettone

Café" in Randpark Ridge is a must-visit. This lively establishment features a dedicated play area equipped with slides, climbing frames, and other exciting attractions to keep little ones entertained while you enjoy your meal. The menu offers a range of options, including pizzas, pastas, and decadent desserts. It's the perfect spot for families looking to enjoy a relaxed meal while the kids burn off some energy.

Depending on the age of your children, it's worth checking if the restaurant offers amenities such as highchairs, baby-changing stations, or child-friendly utensils. These small details can make a big difference in ensuring a comfortable dining experience for everyone.

While many family-friendly restaurants provide entertainment for kids, it's a good idea to bring along small toys, coloring books, or games to keep your little ones engaged during any potential waiting times.

Family dining is all about creating lasting memories. Embrace the joy and excitement of dining out with your loved ones. Take the time to connect, laugh, and share experiences over a delicious meal. It's these precious moments that truly make family adventures memorable.

41. DISHES FOR THE BRAVE

If you're seeking unique culinary experiences in Johannesburg, get ready to tantalize your taste buds with some daring dishes that will test your bravery. Do you want to test your culinary boundaries? Well Johannesburg is the perfect place to do this!

Let's start with "Mopane Worms," a dish that will surely separate the adventurous eaters from the faint of heart. I have never tried these but apparently, they are protein-packed delicacies made from caterpillar larvae harvested from mopane trees. This delicacy can be found in various establishments and markets across Johannesburg. Mopane worms are deep-fried or sautéed with spices to create a unique and savory snack. While their appearance may seem intimidating, many locals and curious foodies find them surprisingly delicious. I don't know about you, but I will pass on this one!

One popular tripe dish you'll encounter in Johannesburg is "tripe stew," also known as "tripe and trotters." This dish is made by slow cooking the tripe and trotters (feet) in a flavorful broth with spices and vegetables. The long cooking process allows the flavors to meld together, resulting in tender tripe and rich, flavorful gravy. It's often served with pap or rice, and for the adventurous people who are brave enough to try it, provides a wholesome meal.

If you're feeling extra adventurous then, "Walkie Talkies" should be on your list. This peculiar dish consists of chicken feet and heads, cooked in a spicy sauce until tender. Walkie Talkies are typically braised or fried and are popular street food in Johannesburg's townships. They are known for their unique texture and intense flavor. You can find them at local food markets and informal eateries if you are up for the challenge!

Now, let's talk about "Skop," a dish that might make you raise an eyebrow. Skop, also known as "sheep's head," is a traditional delicacy enjoyed in many South African communities, including Johannesburg. The sheep's head is boiled until the meat is tender and then served with pap and vegetables. While the sight of a whole sheep's head may be intimidating, you will find many locals who appreciate the succulent meat and interesting textures that come with this unique dish. To experience Skop, head to authentic African restaurants or local eateries that embrace traditional cuisine.

Trying new and daring dishes is all about embracing the unknown. Approach these unique delicacies with an open mind and a sense of adventure. Easier said than done, but you never know, you might discover a new favorite!

Remember that some of these unique dishes may be an acquired taste, so take your time and savor each bite. Start with small portions and gradually build up your adventurous appetite. Many of these dishes come with condiments or accompaniments that enhance the flavors. Experiment with different sauces, chutneys, or side dishes to find the perfect combination that suits your palate.

Remember, the journey of culinary exploration is about stepping out of your comfort zone, embracing new flavors, and immersing yourself in the local culture. So, muster up your courage, put on your adventurous hat, and let Johannesburg's daring dishes ignite your taste buds with their unique flavors and textures. Take pictures because you never know when you are going to encounter these foods again!

42. FOR THE NIGHT OWL AND THE EARLY BIRD

If you find yourself craving a bite to eat in the wee hours of the morning or late at night, Johannesburg has got you covered. The city has a variety of eateries that keep their doors open 24 hours, ensuring you never have to go hungry, no matter the time.

First stop, "The Local Diner" in Melville. This iconic diner is a favorite among locals and night owls looking for a hearty meal at any hour. Located in the lively neighborhood of Melville, The Local Diner serves up classic American-style comfort food with a South African twist. Whether you're craving a juicy burger, a plate of fluffy pancakes, or an omelet, this diner has you covered. The laid-back atmosphere and friendly staff make it the perfect spot to satisfy those late-night cravings, especially after a night out in the town!

For a taste of authentic Turkish cuisine, look no further than "Anatoli" in Greenpoint. This popular 24-hour restaurant is a haven for food enthusiasts who appreciate the rich flavors and textures of Turkish dishes. From succulent kebabs to mezze platters, Anatoli offers its visitors a diverse menu that caters to all taste buds.

If you're craving something sweet in the late hours, "Waffle House" in Norwood is well worth the trip. This 24-hour eatery specializes in waffles that are sure to satisfy your sweet tooth. From classic Belgian waffles topped with fresh fruit and whipped cream to indulgent creations drizzled with chocolate sauce, Waffle House offers a wide range of options to fulfill your dessert cravings.

For those who prefer a variety of options under one roof, "Montecasino" in Fourways is a hub of 24-hour eateries and entertainment. This popular complex is home to numerous restaurants and cafes that cater to all tastes and cravings. Whether you're in the mood for pizza, sushi, burgers, or even gelato, you'll find it all at Montecasino. The lively atmosphere and diverse dining options make it a great place to gather with friends or simply indulge in a late-night feast.

While these eateries are open 24 hours, it's always a good idea to check their current operating hours or any temporary closures, just to be sure. Also bear in mind that when venturing out late at night you ensure you travel in well-lit areas and take necessary precautions to stay safe. If possible, use reputable transportation services or travel with a group of friends.

Use the opportunity to explore different neighborhoods and discover hidden gems that offer late-night dining options. With so many 24-hour eateries at your disposal, you can satisfy your cravings at any time of the day or night in Johannesburg.

43. THE NIGHT CAP

If you're looking to unwind and indulge in the vibrant bar scene of Johannesburg, you're in for a treat. This city is brimming with establishments that offer unique and delicious alcoholic beverages, coupled with a lively atmosphere and various food options.

"The Immigrant Bar" in Braamfontein is trendy bar that celebrates the diversity of Johannesburg through its innovative cocktail menu that features locally inspired drinks. From Rooibos-infused cocktails to craft beers brewed in the nearby neighborhoods, The Immigrant Bar offers a true taste of Johannesburg. Pair your drink with their delicious tapas-style menu, which includes South African favorites like boerewors bites and peri-peri chicken skewers.

"Sin+Tax" in Rosebank is a stylish bar, known for its inventive cocktails that incorporate indigenous ingredients and flavors. Sip on a "Joburg Jam Jar" infused with local fruit and craft spirits or indulge in a "Mzansi Mule" that features the unique flavors of ginger beer and local botanicals. The bar also offers a delectable food menu, featuring small plates and shareable dishes that complement the drinks perfectly.

Do you want a beer? If you're a fan of craft beer, you can't miss "The Mad Giant Brewery" in Newtown. This brewery is perfect for beer enthusiasts and offers its customers a a range of handcrafted brews that showcase the diversity and creativity of Johannesburg's beer scene. From hoppy IPAs to smooth stouts, their beer menu will impress even the most discerning palate. Pair your brew with their mouthwatering gourmet burgers or artisanal pizzas for a complete and satisfying experience.

For a taste of the city's vibrant nightlife, head to "Randlords" in Braamfontein. This rooftop bar offers panoramic views of Johannesburg's skyline, creating a stunning backdrop for an unforgettable evening. I will attest to the fact that this place is amazing! You can sip on their signature cocktails or indulge in an extensive selection of local wines and spirits. The bar also offers a great food menu, featuring a fusion of international and local flavors. Enjoy dishes like springbok carpaccio, bobotie spring rolls, or braai-style grilled meats, while you enjoy the breathtaking views of the city.

In the mood for a lively and energetic atmosphere? "Hell's Kitchen" in Melville is the place to be. This rock 'n' roll-themed bar exudes a rebellious spirit and is known for its craft cocktails and extensive whiskey selection. From classic Old Fashioneds to innovative whiskey-based creations, the bar offers a wide range of options to suit every taste. Pair your drink with their delicious bar bites, such as loaded nachos or gourmet sliders, for a satisfying evening!

Johannesburg's bars offer a unique opportunity to indulge in drinks that incorporate indigenous ingredients and flavors so try to be open to trying something new and embracing the local twists on classic cocktails.

Don't forget to eat! Many of these bars also offer delectable food options that complement their drink menus. Take the time to explore the culinary offerings and indulge in the delicious dishes on offer. It's the perfect way to balance out the drinks and enhance your overall experience.

Probably, the most important tip I am going to give you is to make sure that you do not drink and drive. Johannesburg police take drinking and driving very seriously, so it is a good idea to make sure that you have your mobile with you to order an Uber or choose a designated driver that is happy not to drink alcohol for the night. Remember, safety should always come first!

44. JOHANNESBURG FARMERS MARKETS

Are you in the mood for something a little different? Why not take a memorable adventure through Johannesburg's vibrant farmers markets? Let me tell you about some of the best spots to purchase local fresh produce, artisanal goods, and mouthwatering cuisine.

For those venturing into the Fourways neighborhood, the Fourways Farmers Market is a must-visit. Every Sunday, this market pays homage to the region's agricultural heritage and offers a vibrant space filled with farm-fresh produce and unique crafts. As you wander through the stalls, you'll be amazed by the variety and quality of the offerings. From organic fruits and vegetables to handmade cheeses, preserves, and freshly baked goods, it's a food lover's paradise. After browsing through the stalls, you can take a break from shopping and treat yourself to some treats from the food stalls. Whether you're craving wood-fired pizza, gourmet burgers, or farm-to-table delights, there is something at this market for everyone.

If you're up for a short trip outside Johannesburg, head to the Irene Village Market in Centurion. This market, held on the first and last Saturday of each month, is filled with arts, crafts, and delicious food. As you wander through the stalls, you'll discover an incredible range of handcrafted goods, homemade treats, and fresh produce. Fill your basket with organic vegetables, specialty breads, and local cheeses.

Last but certainly not least, make your way to the Hazel Food Market in Pretoria, just a short drive from Johannesburg. The Hazel Food market is open on Saturdays and showcases a variety of food offerings that will leave you spoilt for choice. Take your time to explore the stalls and savor the flavors of the carefully crafted dishes. Whether you're in the mood for gourmet sandwiches, vegan treats, or artisanal baked goods, Hazel Food Market has it all.

As you embark on your journey through Johannesburg's farmers markets, keep a few tips in mind. Arrive early to beat the crowds and secure the freshest produce. Don't be shy to strike up conversations with vendors, as they love sharing their stories and knowledge. And most importantly, embrace the vibrant atmosphere and let your taste buds guide you on a culinary adventure.

So, get ready to explore the flavors, aromas, and vibrant energy of Johannesburg's farmers markets. Immerse yourself in the local culture, support local producers, and savor the abundance of fresh and delicious offerings. Happy market hopping!

45. READY FOR A SCARE?

I would like to tell you about something a little different. If you feel like a spine-tingling journey through the mysterious side of Johannesburg, you must book a seat on the thrilling Johannesburg Ghost Tours! If you're a fan of paranormal tales, historical mysteries, and a good scare, this is the perfect adventure for you.

The Johannesburg Ghost Tours offer a unique and immersive experience, taking you on a guided tour to some of the city's most haunted locations. As darkness falls, the bus winds its way through the atmospheric streets, transporting you to a world of ghostly tales and unexplained phenomena.

One of the highlights of this ghost tour is a visit to the notorious Old Fort Prison Complex, also known as Number Four. This historical site holds a dark past and is said to be haunted by the spirits of its former prisoners. While you explore the eerie corridors and cells, your guide will share bone-chilling stories of the inmates and the paranormal encounters reported by its visitors. The next stop on the tour is the mysterious Johannesburg Park Station. With its long history and numerous reported ghostly sightings, this iconic transportation hub has become a hotbed of supernatural activity.

As you venture through the haunted sites, your tour guide will regale you with tales of Johannesburg's past, weaving together history, folklore, and paranormal encounters. You'll learn about the city's dark secrets, unsolved mysteries, and the restless spirits that are said to wander the streets of Johannesburg!

Enough of the scary stuff, let's talk about the divine cuisine that accompanies this eerie adventure. After all, exploring haunted locations can work up quite an appetite! Along the tour route, you'll have the opportunity to taste cuisine that captures the essence of Johannesburg's ghostly vibe.

Upon stepping into a haunted-themed restaurant, where you'll be served dishes inspired by local legends with their own ghostly tales. Sink your teeth into a "Spectral Steak," a perfectly cooked piece of meat that seems to melt in your mouth, or why not try a "Phantom Pasta," a tantalizing dish infused with flavors that linger long after each bite.

If you have a sweet tooth, there are spine-tingling desserts that will send shivers down your spine such as the "Ghoul's Delight," a decadent chocolate creation or the "Wicked Witch's Waffles," topped with delicious flavors! Of course, no ghostly culinary experience would be complete without a hauntingly good drink. Sip on a "Spectral Spirit," a mysterious concoction that seems to change flavors with each sip or order a "Ghastly Goblet" filled with chillingly refreshing ingredients.

While the Johannesburg Ghost Tours provide an exhilarating and spooky experience, it's important to remember that the stories and legends shared are meant for entertainment purposes. Whether you believe in the supernatural or not, the tour offers a unique way to explore the city's history and enjoy some deliciously eerie cuisine along the way.

Remember to dress comfortably, but also consider embracing the spirit of the tour by adding a touch of eerie attire to your ensemble. Bring along a jacket or sweater, as some tour stops may be outdoors, and the evenings can get chilly. And don't forget your camera! You never know when you might capture an otherworldly image or encounter a strange phenomenon. To fully immerse yourself in the experience, listen attentively to the tales and let your imagination run wild. Engage with the stories, ask questions, and allow yourself to be captivated by the supernatural narratives. I have been on The Johannesburg Ghost Tour twice, and it does not disappoint. I do, however, feel that this may not be suitable for children under 12.

46. THE JOHANNESBURG TOUR BUS

Ah, the Johannesburg tour bus! This is an iconic and convenient way for tourists to explore the vibrant city. Hop on board and get ready for an adventure filled with sightseeing, cultural discoveries, and of course, delightful cuisine.

The Johannesburg tour bus, often known as the "Hop-On Hop-Off" bus, is a popular mode of transportation for tourists seeking a comprehensive overview of the city's landmarks, attractions, and hidden gems. The bus follows a carefully curated route, allowing you to hop on and off at various stops at your own pace. It's a fantastic way to navigate the city, especially if you're short of time or prefer a hassle-free exploration experience.

The bus takes you through the bustling streets of Johannesburg, passing by iconic landmarks such as Constitution Hill, the Apartheid Museum, and the Nelson Mandela Square. During the drive you will be treated to fascinating commentary that brings the city's history, culture, and heritage to life.

The bus conveniently stops at locations where you can indulge in delicious cuisine representing the diverse flavors of Johannesburg. Consider hopping off at the vibrant Maboneng Precinct, where you'll find an array of trendy cafes, street food stalls, and international restaurants.

As the bus continues its journey, you'll pass by the vibrant Newtown area where you can explore the Market Theatre Complex, a cultural hotspot that often hosts food festivals and events showcasing local and international cuisines. Here, you can treat yourself to a delicious meal while enjoying the artistic ambiance of the area.

If you're looking for a taste of traditional South African cuisine, hop off at Soweto, the famous township on the outskirts of Johannesburg. This culturally rich neighborhood is home to vibrant shebeens (local bars) and restaurants where you can savor authentic dishes like boerewors, samp and beans, and chakalaka. To satisfy your sweet tooth, consider why not hop off near Melville and try some delectable pastries or freshly brewed coffee as you take a break from the tour.

Throughout your tour, keep in mind that the Johannesburg tour bus offers the flexibility to hop on and off at your leisure. Plan your stops. Before hopping on the tour bus, take some time to research the stops along the route and identify the culinary hotspots you'd like to explore. This will help you maximize your time and ensure you don't miss out on any must-try restaurants or food stalls.

It is also important to take note of timing. Consider the time of day when planning your bus adventure. Some restaurants or food stalls may have specific opening hours or may be busier during certain times. If there's a particular eatery that you are keen to visit, it's worth checking their operating hours in advance to avoid disappointment.

47. WE ALL SCREAM FOR ICE CREAM

If like me you are a fan of frozen treats and indulgent desserts, you're in for a sweet adventure. Join me as we explore the best ice cream parlors in the city, discover their unique offerings, and satisfy our cravings with delectable scoops of frozen delight.

First up on our ice cream escapade is "Scoop & Smile," a charming ice cream parlor located in the heart of downtown Johannesburg. As you step inside, you're greeted by the aroma of freshly made waffle cones and the sight of colorful ice cream tubs lining the counter. There are so many flavors to choose from, from classic flavors like vanilla and chocolate to innovative creations like salted caramel swirl and cookies and cream. I strongly suggest that you don’t miss their specialty sundae, the "Ultimate Dream," which features a medley of ice cream flavors, toppings, and a cherry on top.

"The Creamery," is another popular ice cream destination nestled in the trendy neighborhood of Melville. With its rustic decor and cozy ambiance, this artisanal ice cream parlor offers a delectable range of flavors made with locally sourced ingredients. Indulge in their signature flavor, "Melville Malt," a creamy blend of malted milk and chocolate, or try the refreshing "Lemon Curd & Ginger" for a zesty twist. Don't forget to pair your scoops with their homemade waffle cones or treat yourself to a mouthwatering ice cream sandwich!

Situated in the vibrant district of Rosebank, “Frozen Fusions” offers an array of exciting options, including liquid nitrogen ice cream. From exotic flavors like passionfruit and lychee to indulgent choices like triple chocolate brownie, "Frozen Fusions" is a dream for ice cream enthusiasts seeking a one-of-a-kind experience.

For those seeking a touch of nostalgia, our next stop is "The Vintage Scoop," a retro-inspired ice cream parlor located in the bustling neighborhood of Parkhurst. Step into a bygone era as you admire the vintage decor and sample their selection of classic ice cream flavors. Their banana splits served in a vintage dish are to die for. The highlight of "The Vintage Scoop" is their hand-spun milkshakes, made with premium ice cream and served in old-fashioned glasses. One for the books!

As you embark on your ice cream escapades, keep in mind a few tips to enhance your experience. Check the opening hours of the ice cream parlors before visiting, as some may have varying schedules. Consider trying a variety of flavors to fully appreciate the creativity and craftsmanship of each establishment. And, of course, don't be afraid to indulge in some toppings or extra treats to make your ice cream adventure even more indulgent.

Many ice cream parlors in Johannesburg pride themselves on using locally sourced ingredients and incorporating South African flavors into their offerings. Be sure to inquire about any specialty flavors or ice cream creations that showcase the region's unique culinary heritage. By trying these local specialties, you'll get a taste of the vibrant and diverse food culture of Johannesburg.

And lastly, take your time! Brain freeze is real! Ice cream is meant to be savored and enjoyed at a leisurely pace. Instead of rushing through your treat, find a comfortable spot within the ice cream parlor or nearby park to sit back, relax, and savor each spoonful.

48. ROMANCE IN JOHANNESBURG

Romance is in the air! Let me take you on a journey through some of the most enchanting and romantic establishments in Johannesburg, where you can create beautiful memories with your loved one. From intimate dining experiences to dreamy settings, Johannesburg has plenty to offer for a truly romantic evening.

For a magical dining experience with breathtaking views, look no further than Flames Restaurant at the Four Seasons Hotel. This hotel is located on a hilltop, offering panoramic vistas of the city skyline and stunning gardens. You and your other half can have a romantic candlelit dinner on the terrace, where you can savor a variety of culinary delights from their menu. Choose from the restaurants grilled seafood to succulent steaks and soak in the romantic ambiance.

For a unique blend of romance, history, and culture, visit The Pot Luck Club in the trendy suburb of Braamfontein. Located on the rooftop of the iconic Museum of African Design, this restaurant offers stunning views of the city skyline. The eclectic menu features tapas-style dishes inspired by flavors from around the world, allowing you to explore a variety of tastes together. The chic and contemporary setting, paired with the panoramic views, creates an ambiance that is both romantic and stylish.

Bellagio is a renowned restaurant located in the picturesque suburb of Westcliff in Johannesburg. It is well-regarded for its romantic ambiance and stunning views, making it a popular choice for couples seeking a memorable dining experience. The romantic atmosphere at Bellagio is created by its elegant interior design and its prime location overlooking the Johannesburg skyline. When it comes to cuisine, Bellagio offers a delightful mix of Mediterranean and continental dishes with a focus on fresh, high-quality ingredients. Overall, Bellagio in Westcliff offers a romantic and enchanting setting, coupled with a delectable Mediterranean-inspired cuisine. It's an ideal choice for a special date night or an anniversary celebration, where you can enjoy exquisite food, breathtaking views, and the company of your loved one.

As you embark on your romantic adventures in Johannesburg, keep a few tips in mind. Make reservations in advance to secure your preferred spot, especially during peak times or special occasions. Dress to impress and embrace the ambiance of each establishment.

Consider the logistics of getting to and from your chosen romantic establishment. If you're not familiar with the area or prefer not to drive, opt for a reputable taxi service or ride-hailing app like Uber or Bolt. This way, you can relax and enjoy the evening without worrying about navigation or parking.

Plan your visit during a time that suits your preferences. If you prefer a quieter and more intimate atmosphere, consider going on a weeknight or earlier in the evening. On the other hand, if you enjoy a livelier ambiance, opt for weekends or special event nights when the venue may offer live music or entertainment.

If you're celebrating a special occasion, such as an anniversary or birthday, inform the establishment in advance. Many restaurants are happy to accommodate special requests or provide personalized touches to make the evening even more memorable. Whether it's a personalized dessert or a special message on a menu, these small gestures can make a big difference.

49. WHAT FOODS YOU CAN TAKE BACK HOME WITH YOU?

Are you thinking of bringing a a piece of Johannesburg's culinary delights back home with you? There are indeed some fantastic food products that you can take with you as a delicious reminder of your time in this vibrant city. So, let me guide you through some of the food products that are worth considering for your culinary journey back home.

One iconic product you mustn't miss is biltong, a popular South African dried and cured meat. It comes in various flavors like beef, game, or even ostrich. Biltong is a perfect snack to enjoy on-the-go or to share with friends and family. You can find high-quality biltong in specialty stores or local markets throughout Johannesburg. Just make sure to check the import regulations of your home country to ensure you can bring it back without any issues.

If you have a sweet tooth, be sure to stock up on some delicious South African chocolates. Cadbury Dairy Milk is a favorite amongst locals, and you can find unique flavors like Top Deck (a blend of milk and white chocolate) or Astros (chocolate-covered caramel and biscuit balls). Look out for locally made artisanal chocolates as well, which often showcase a fusion of African flavors and European chocolate-making techniques. These sweet delights will surely bring a smile to your face and make for a delightful gift.

When it comes to savory delights, consider taking home some unique South African spices and sauces. Peri-Peri sauce, known for its spicy kick, is a must-try condiment that adds a fiery flavor to any dish. You can find it in supermarkets or specialty food stores in Johannesburg. Also, keep an eye out for Cape Malay curry spice blends, which feature a fragrant mix of spices that reflect the diverse cultural heritage of South Africa. These spices and sauces will allow you to recreate the flavors of Johannesburg in your own kitchen.

Before purchasing food products to take home, familiarize yourself with the import regulations of your home country. Different countries have varying rules and restrictions regarding the importation of food items. Visit the official website of your country's customs or border protection agency to understand the specific requirements and limitations.

When going through customs, it's essential to truthfully declare any food items you are bringing with you. Some countries have strict rules regarding the importation of certain food products, particularly fresh produce, meat, or dairy. By declaring your items, you are ensuring compliance with the regulations and avoiding potential fines or confiscation of prohibited goods.

When packing food products for your journey, ensure they are properly sealed and packaged to prevent any leaks or spoilage. Consider using airtight containers or resealable bags to maintain freshness and prevent odors from permeating other items in your luggage. It's also a good idea to separate any liquids or sauces from solid items to avoid potential spills.

50. HOW TO PAY

When it comes to paying for your purchases in Johannesburg, you'll find that most establishments are well-equipped to handle various payment methods. Whether you prefer using cash or relying on your trusty credit or debit card, you'll have plenty of options to make transactions convenient and hassle-free.

First and foremost, it's important to note that card payments are widely accepted throughout Johannesburg. The city is equipped with a robust banking infrastructure and advanced payment systems, making it easy to swipe, tap, or insert your card for purchases. From supermarkets and malls to restaurants, hotels, and tourist attractions, you'll find that card payments are the norm.

Carrying cash is still advisable for smaller vendors, street markets, and situations where card payment may not be available. However, it's always a good idea to have a mix of cash and cards to cater to different payment scenarios. ATMs are readily available throughout the city, allowing you to withdraw cash whenever needed.

Major credit cards such as Visa and Mastercard are widely accepted in Johannesburg. You'll find card payment terminals at most establishments, where you can simply insert or tap your card and enter your PIN to complete the transaction. Contactless payment methods, such as mobile wallets and smart cards, are also becoming increasingly popular, so you may have the option to pay with your smartphone or wearable device.

It's worth noting that some establishments may have a minimum spending requirement for card payments, so it's helpful to have some cash on hand for smaller purchases. However, this is less common in larger establishments and popular tourist areas.

In addition to card payments, online and mobile banking services have gained significant popularity in Johannesburg. Many locals use mobile banking apps to transfer funds, pay bills, and make online purchases. While tourists may not have access to local banking apps, you can still rely on your own mobile banking app or online payment platforms to make secure transactions.

So, go ahead and explore Johannesburg with peace of mind, knowing that you can conveniently pay for your items using your preferred payment method. Just remember to keep an eye out for card payment terminals, and don't hesitate to ask if you're unsure about the accepted payment methods at a specific establishment. Happy shopping and dining!

BONUS TIPS

I do hope that this book has helped you to gain some insight into the beautiful city of Johannesburg, a city that I am proud to call my home. As you bid farewell to Johannesburg, may the memories of its vibrant streets, diverse culture, and warm hospitality linger in your heart, forever beckoning you to return to my extraordinary home city. In case I have missed anything out, I would like to recap on some bonus tips for your visit to Johannesburg.

WHAT ARE THE TOP 10 HOLIDAYS DESTINATIONS IN JOHANNESBURG?

These destinations provide diverse experiences, from cultural immersion to wildlife encounters, natural beauty, and historical insights. They offer opportunities to explore beyond the bustling city and discover the richness of the surrounding areas. Remember to plan your visits in advance, check opening hours, and consider transportation options to make the most of your holiday experiences in and around Johannesburg.

Here are ten popular holiday destinations near Johannesburg that tourists often explore:

Soweto: Known for its historical significance and vibrant culture, Soweto offers visitors a chance to explore iconic landmarks like the Mandela House and Vilakazi Street, which was once home to Nelson Mandela.

The Cradle of Humankind: A UNESCO World Heritage Site, located just outside Johannesburg, where visitors can explore fascinating caves and learn about human evolution and archaeological discoveries.

Pretoria: South Africa's administrative capital, Pretoria, is known for its beautiful gardens, historical landmarks, and museums. The Union Buildings, Voortrekker Monument, and Pretoria National Botanical Garden are popular attractions.

Magaliesberg Mountains: A picturesque mountain range near Johannesburg, offering opportunities for hiking, rock climbing, and outdoor activities. Visitors can also enjoy hot air balloon rides or explore the quaint towns in the area.

Sun City: A popular resort complex located about two hours from Johannesburg, offering luxurious accommodations, a variety of entertainment options, golf courses, water parks, and wildlife experiences.

Pilanesberg National Park: Adjacent to Sun City, Pilanesberg is a game reserve known for its diverse wildlife, including the Big Five (lion, elephant, rhino, leopard, and buffalo). Visitors can go on safaris and enjoy the beauty of the African bush.

Cradle Moon Lakeside Game Lodge: A nature reserve and lodge located on the outskirts of Johannesburg, offering game drives, birdwatching, fishing, and beautiful scenery. It's a tranquil escape from the city.

Lesedi Cultural Village: A cultural village that showcases the traditions and customs of various South African tribes. Visitors can learn about indigenous cultures, participate in traditional dances, and enjoy authentic African cuisine.

Hartebeespoort Dam: A scenic dam and resort town located close to Johannesburg. It offers activities like boat cruises, cable car rides, craft markets, and waterfront dining.

Cullinan Diamond Mine: A historic diamond mine located near Pretoria, where visitors can take underground tours, learn about diamond mining, and even try their luck at gemstone panning.

WHAT ARE THE TOP 10 DRINKS TO TRY IN JOHANNESBURG?

In Johannesburg, you'll find a wide range of refreshing and unique drinks to quench your thirst and tantalize your taste buds. From traditional favorites to trendy creations, here are ten drinks you should consider trying when visiting Johannesburg:

Start your day with a comforting cup of Rooibos Latte, made with the famous South African herbal tea, rooibos. This caffeine-free beverage offers a smooth and creamy flavor, often topped with a sprinkle of cinnamon or a drizzle of honey.

Indulge in a sweet treat by sipping on an Amarula Dom Pedro. This delightful cocktail combines Amarula cream liqueur, vanilla ice cream, and a splash of chocolate syrup, creating a rich and creamy concoction.

Johannesburg has a booming craft beer scene, with a variety of local breweries offering unique and flavorful beers. From hoppy IPAs to rich stouts and refreshing lagers, beer enthusiasts can explore the city's numerous craft beer bars and breweries.

Immerse yourself in the flavors of Africa with cocktails that showcase indigenous ingredients. Try the Marula Martini, made with the iconic Marula fruit, or the African Mule, a twist on the classic Moscow Mule using local ingredients like ginger beer and Amarula.

Embark on a taste adventure with Mampoer, a traditional South African distilled fruit brandy. This potent spirit comes in various fruit flavors like peach, apricot, and apple, offering a unique and intense drinking experience.

Warm up with a fragrant cup of Chai Latte, a spiced tea blended with steamed milk. This comforting drink combines the flavors of black tea, cinnamon, cardamom, cloves, and ginger, creating a cozy and aromatic beverage.

Refresh yourself with the zingy and invigorating flavors of homemade Ginger Beer. This non-alcoholic beverage is made by fermenting fresh ginger, sugar, and lemon juice. It's perfect for those hot Johannesburg days.

Join the gin revolution by sampling the vibrant craft gin scene in Johannesburg. Enjoy a classic G&T or experiment with unique botanical combinations that showcase local flavors like buchu, rooibos, or citrus fruits.

As South Africa's signature red wine, Pinotage is a must-try for wine enthusiasts. This robust and full-bodied wine offers a distinctive flavor profile with notes of plum, red berries, and smoky undertones.

Johannesburg is blessed with an abundance of delicious fruits, and enjoying a glass of freshly squeezed juice is a delightful way to savor their flavors. Try exotic fruits like mango, guava, or papaya, or opt for classic favorites like orange or grapefruit.

Remember to drink responsibly and pace yourself when trying new beverages. Whether you're exploring trendy bars, cozy cafes, or local markets, Johannesburg offers a diverse array of drinks that capture the spirit and flavors of this vibrant city.

WHAT ARE THE TOP 10 FOODS TO TRY IN JOHANNESBURG?

When it comes to culinary delights, Johannesburg offers a vibrant food scene that caters to a variety of tastes. From traditional South African dishes to international flavors, here are ten must-try foods in Johannesburg:

Indulge in the quintessential South African dining experience with a hearty braai. Sample succulent grilled meats like boerewors (spicy sausage), sosaties (marinated skewered meat), and juicy steaks. Pair it with sides like pap (maize porridge) and chakalaka (spicy vegetable relish) for a complete feast.

A unique street food originating from Durban, Bunny Chow is a hollowed-out loaf of bread filled with delicious curry. Choose from various fillings like chicken, beef, or vegetable curry, and enjoy this flavorsome and filling dish.

Dive into the flavors of South Africa's Cape Malay cuisine with Bobotie, a spiced mince meat dish topped with a custard-like mixture and baked until golden. It's a savory and aromatic delight that combines sweet, savory, and spicy flavors.

This classic South African dish consists of pap (maize porridge) served with tender meat, often accompanied by a tomato and onion relish. It's a hearty and satisfying meal that reflects the country's culinary heritage.

Indulge your sweet tooth with Koeksisters, a traditional South African dessert made of twisted dough that's deep-fried and drenched in a sticky syrup. These syrup-soaked treats are irresistible and perfect for those with a sweet craving.

A popular Cape Town creation that has made its way to Johannesburg, the Gatsby is a massive sandwich filled with various fillings like steak, chicken, or seafood, along with fries and sauces. It's a filling and flavorful street food delight.

Bite into a piping hot Vetkoek, a deep-fried dough bread that can be enjoyed sweet or savory. Try it with a generous filling of curried mince, cheese, or jam for a delightful and satisfying treat.

Satisfy your sweet tooth with Melktert, a traditional South African milk tart. This creamy custard-like tart is made with a sweet pastry crust and a delicate cinnamon-infused milk filling. It's a beloved dessert that pairs perfectly with a cup of tea or coffee.

A favorite snack among South Africans, Biltong is dried and cured meat, typically made from beef or game. It's seasoned with various spices and enjoyed as a protein-packed snack, perfect for on-the-go or a tasty nibble during social gatherings.

End your culinary adventure with a comforting serving of Malva Pudding. This sticky, sweet, and decadent dessert is a sponge-like cake drenched in a warm buttery syrup, often served with custard or vanilla ice cream.

These are just a taste of the diverse flavors Johannesburg has to offer. From traditional South African dishes to culinary fusions and international cuisine, the city is a melting pot of delicious delights. So, get ready to explore the vibrant food scene and savor the mouthwatering flavors of Johannesburg.

THE TOP 10 SOUVENIR TO GET IN JOHANNESBURG?

When visiting Johannesburg, you'll find a variety of unique and memorable souvenirs to take home as a reminder of your time in the city. Here are ten top souvenirs to consider:

Johannesburg is a treasure trove of African art and crafts. Look for hand-carved wooden sculptures, beaded jewelry, intricate baskets, colorful fabrics, and vibrant paintings created by talented local artisans.

South Africa is known for its rich gold and diamond mining heritage. Consider purchasing a piece of beautifully crafted jewelry adorned with locally sourced gold or diamonds, showcasing the country's wealth of natural resources.

Immerse yourself in the rhythms of Africa by bringing home an African drum. These beautifully crafted instruments are not only decorative but also functional, allowing you to create your own beats and melodies.

Support local artists by purchasing vibrant and expressive paintings or sculptures that reflect the spirit of Johannesburg's townships. These art pieces capture the essence of South African culture and make for eye-catching souvenirs.

Zulu beadwork is a traditional art form celebrated in South Africa. Look for beaded keychains, bracelets, necklaces, or even beaded animal figurines that showcase the intricate and colorful beadwork of the Zulu people.

Johannesburg has a rich literary tradition, and you can find an array of books by South African authors.

Consider picking up novels, poetry collections, or non-fiction works that offer insights into the country's history, culture, or social issues.

Explore the unique sounds of Africa by bringing home a traditional musical instrument such as a kalimba (thumb piano), marimba, or mbira. These instruments allow you to continue the musical journey even after you leave Johannesburg.

Vibrant and colorful African fabrics are a must-have souvenir. Look for fabrics like Shweshwe or Ankara that can be used to create unique clothing, accessories, or even home decor items.

South Africa is renowned for its incredible wildlife. Look for souvenirs inspired by these majestic creatures, such as hand-carved animal figurines, beaded animal keychains, or wildlife-themed artwork.

South Africa is known for its exceptional wines and spirits. Consider bringing home a bottle or two of locally produced wine, brandy, or Amarula cream liqueur to enjoy and share with friends and family.

Remember, when purchasing souvenirs, look for reputable shops, markets, or galleries that support local artisans and communities. These souvenirs not only represent the unique culture and heritage of Johannesburg but also serve as lasting reminders of your memorable journey through the city and its surroundings.

MUST TAKE PICTURES IN JOHANNESBURG?

When exploring Johannesburg, there are numerous picturesque spots that are worth capturing with your camera. Here are some must-take pictures to help you preserve the memories of your visit:

Snap a photo of the iconic Nelson Mandela Bridge, which is not only a significant landmark but also a symbol of unity in South Africa.

Visit Vilakazi Street in Soweto, the only street in the world that was home to two Nobel Prize laureates, Nelson Mandela and Archbishop Desmond Tutu. Capture the vibrant atmosphere and colorful houses.

Take a picture of the striking Constitutional Court building, known for its unique architecture and historical significance as a symbol of justice and democracy in South Africa.

Explore the vibrant Maboneng Precinct and photograph the colorful street art and graffiti that adorns the walls, reflecting the creative spirit of Johannesburg.

Capture the powerful exhibits and poignant displays at the Apartheid Museum, documenting the history and struggle for freedom in South Africa.

Visit the Lion Park and capture the majestic lions up close in their natural habitat. Take a selfie with these magnificent creatures in the background (from a safe distance, of course).

Explore the beautiful Walter Sisulu National Botanical Garden and photograph the stunning waterfall cascading into the lush surroundings.

Visit the Market on Main in Maboneng and capture the bustling atmosphere, unique crafts, and delicious street food offerings.

Head to one of the rooftop bars or viewpoints and capture the panoramic view of the Johannesburg skyline, showcasing the city's impressive architecture and urban landscape.

Take a hike at Melville Koppies Nature Reserve and capture the breathtaking views of the city from atop the ancient geological formation.

Remember, photography is a wonderful way to capture the essence and beauty of Johannesburg, but it's equally important to be respectful of the places you visit and the people you encounter. Always follow any photography guidelines or restrictions and be mindful of the privacy of individuals when taking pictures. Enjoy your photography adventure in Johannesburg and create lasting memories of your time in the city.

TOP 10 SITES TO SEE IN JOHANNESBURG?

When visiting Johannesburg, there are many attractions and sites to explore that showcase the city's rich history, culture, and natural beauty. Here are ten must-visit sites in Johannesburg:

Apartheid Museum: Delve into the history of apartheid and the struggle for freedom at this powerful museum. It offers a comprehensive and thought-provoking experience.

Nelson Mandela Square: Pay homage to the iconic leader at Nelson Mandela Square, where you'll find a larger-than-life statue of Nelson Mandela surrounded by shops, restaurants, and entertainment.

Constitution Hill: Visit this historic site that once housed a prison and now serves as the Constitutional Court of South Africa. Explore the exhibits and learn about the country's journey towards democracy.

Soweto: Visit the vibrant township of Soweto, home to significant historical sites like the Hector

Pieterson Museum, Vilakazi Street, and the former homes of Nelson Mandela and Archbishop Desmond Tutu.

Cradle of Humankind: Discover the birthplace of humanity at this UNESCO World Heritage Site, located just outside Johannesburg. Explore the ancient fossil sites and underground caves that reveal our human origins.

Johannesburg Botanical Garden: Escape to nature at this serene garden, featuring beautifully landscaped areas, a stunning rose garden, and a variety of indigenous plants. Enjoy a picnic or a leisurely stroll.

The Lion and Safari Park: Experience an up-close encounter with wildlife at this park. Take a safari tour, interact with lion cubs, and even go on a guided walking tour to see cheetahs and other animals.

The Market Theatre: Immerse yourself in the arts at the renowned Market Theatre, known for its groundbreaking productions and commitment to social change. Catch a play, musical, or dance performance.

Maboneng Precinct: This vibrant neighborhood is filled with art galleries, trendy shops, hip cafes, and lively street markets. Marvel at the street art and soak up the creative energy of the area.

Walter Sisulu National Botanical Garden: Enjoy the natural beauty of this botanical garden, known for its stunning waterfall and abundant birdlife. Take a hike, have a picnic, or simply relax in the peaceful surroundings.

These are just a few of the many attractions that Johannesburg has to offer. Remember to plan your visits accordingly and consider guided tours for a deeper understanding of the sites and respect any rules or regulations in place to ensure a safe and enjoyable experience. Explore, discover, and make the most of your time in Johannesburg!

TOP 10 CULTURE SHOCKS WHEN VISITING JOHANNESBURG?

When visiting Johannesburg, tourists may encounter some cultural differences that can be surprising or unfamiliar. Here are ten potential culture shocks that tourists might experience in Johannesburg:

Language Diversity

Johannesburg is a melting pot of cultures and languages. The diversity of languages spoken, including English, Afrikaans, Zulu, and others, may be surprising to some visitors.

Safety Precautions

Johannesburg has certain safety precautions that may differ from what tourists are accustomed to. It is important to be aware of your surroundings, take precautions with personal belongings, and follow local advice regarding safety.

Traffic Congestion

Johannesburg is a bustling city, and traffic congestion is common, especially during peak hours.

The volume of vehicles on the roads can be overwhelming for visitors not accustomed to heavy traffic.

Greeting Customs

South Africans often greet each other with a handshake or hug, and sometimes a kiss on the cheek. This level of physical contact may differ from cultural norms in other countries.

Time Concept

South African time can be more relaxed and flexible compared to other cultures, which may result in more relaxed attitudes towards punctuality or different perceptions of time.

Service in Restaurants

In South Africa, it is customary to call the server when you need assistance or the bill, rather than expecting frequent check-ins from waitstaff. This self-service approach may be different from what some tourists are used to.

Cultural Diversity

Johannesburg is known for its cultural diversity, with various ethnic communities living side by side.

Embracing and respecting this diversity can be an enriching experience for visitors.

Tipping Culture

Tipping is customary in South Africa, and it is polite to leave a gratuity for good service in restaurants, hotels, and for other services. It is helpful to familiarize yourself with the tipping customs to ensure appropriate gratuities.

Water and Power Conservation

South Africa experiences periodic water and power shortages. Visitors may encounter measures such as load shedding (scheduled power outages) or water conservation efforts, which may affect daily routines.

Traditional Cuisine

South African cuisine is diverse and may include dishes that tourists are unfamiliar with, such as tripe, mopane worms, or chakalaka. Trying traditional dishes can be a cultural experience, and it's worth embracing the local cuisine.

Remember, while some of these aspects may initially be surprising, they contribute to the unique cultural experience of visiting Johannesburg. Embrace the differences, be open-minded, and take the opportunity to learn and engage with the local culture. Respect for local customs and an open attitude will go a long way towards making your visit to Johannesburg a memorable and enriching experience.

10 SCAMS I SHOULD LOOK OUT FOR WHEN VISITING

While Johannesburg is a vibrant and exciting city to visit, it's always wise to be aware of potential scams that can occur in any destination. Here are ten common scams to watch out for when visiting Johannesburg:

Be careful when using ATMs and card payment terminals. Skimmers may be used to capture card information, so always cover your PIN and use ATMs in well-lit, secure areas.

Be wary of individuals who try to distract you, such as by spilling something on you or engaging in a lively conversation while their accomplice attempts to steal your belongings.

Be cautious if someone claiming to be a police officer approaches you and asks to see your identification or passport. Ask for official identification and, if in doubt, request assistance from a nearby police station.

Use licensed taxis or ride-hailing services like Uber, and always ensure the meter is used or negotiate a fare upfront. Avoid unmarked or unregistered taxis as they may overcharge or take longer routes.

While most street vendors are legitimate, be cautious of inflated prices or counterfeit goods. Bargain with vendors, but exercise common sense and ensure the safety of your belongings.

Be on the lookout for individuals or groups asking for donations for charity or community projects. If you wish to contribute, research reputable charities, and donate directly to them.

In some cases, there may be individuals that may be posing as tour guides or offering assistance at tourist sites. Stick to licensed tour operators and official information centers for reliable guidance.

Avoid purchasing counterfeit items, such as designer products or electronics, from unauthorized sellers. These products may be of poor quality and illegal to bring back to your home country.

Use reputable car rental companies and carefully inspect the vehicle before renting. Take note of any existing damage and ensure you return the car in the same condition to avoid additional charges.

Book accommodation through reputable websites or directly with established hotels and guesthouses. Be cautious of offers that seem too good to be true and always verify the legitimacy of the property.

Remember, awareness and vigilance are key to avoiding scams. Trust your instincts, research before making any transactions, and seek assistance from trusted sources, such as official tourist information centers or local authorities, if you have any concerns. By staying informed and alert, you can have a safe and enjoyable visit to Johannesburg.

And as the sun sets behind the city's skyline, I whispered, "Come experience Johannesburg's vibrant spirit, warm people, and endless wonders. You'll leave with a piece of my home in your heart."Other

RESOURCES

Here are some links to travel websites, useful phone numbers, apps, and maps of Johannesburg.

TRAVEL WEBSITES:

Lonely Planet - Johannesburg (www.lonelyplanet.com/south-africa/johannesburg): Offers comprehensive travel guides, tips, and recommendations for Johannesburg.

Johannesburg City Guide (www.joburg.co.za): Provides information on attractions, events, restaurants, and accommodations in Johannesburg.

Gauteng Tourism (www.gauteng.net): Official website for tourism in Gauteng province, which includes Johannesburg. It offers detailed information on attractions, activities, and accommodations.

Here are some popular accommodation websites where you can search for hotels, guesthouses, and other types of accommodations in Johannesburg:

Booking.com (www.booking.com)
Expedia (www.expedia.com)
Airbnb (www.airbnb.com)
Hotels.com (www.hotels.com)
Agoda (www.agoda.com)
TripAdvisor (www.tripadvisor.com)
Travelocity (www.travelocity.com)
Trivago (www.trivago.com)
Orbitz (www.orbitz.com)

These websites offer a wide range of options, allowing you to search for accommodations based on your preferences, budget, and desired location in Johannesburg. Make sure to read reviews, compare prices, and check the availability of your chosen accommodations before making a booking.

USEFUL PHONE NUMBERS:

Emergency Services (Police, Ambulance, Fire): 10111
Johannesburg Tourism Information: +27 (0)11 883 8167
OR Tambo International Airport Information: +27 (0)11 921 6262
Gautrain (rapid transit railway service): +27 (0)86 010 5000

Johannesburg Tourism Visitor Information: +27 (0)11 883 8167
O.R. Tambo International Airport Customer Service: +27 (0)11 921 6262
Gautrain Customer Service: +27 (0)86 010 2100

TRAVEL APPS:

Zomato: An app that provides information and reviews of restaurants in Johannesburg, helping you find dining options based on your preferences.

Gautrain App: Official app for the Gautrain service, offering real-time train schedules, ticket purchasing, and service updates.

Uber or Bolt: Ride-hailing apps for convenient transportation.

MAPS OF JOHANNESBURG:

OpenStreetMap (www.openstreetmap.org): A collaborative and open-source mapping platform where you can find maps of Johannesburg. It provides detailed street-level information and can be accessed offline with the right app.

HERE WeGo: A mapping app that offers offline maps of Johannesburg, along with turn-by-turn navigation, public transportation information, and points of interest.

Google Maps: You can search for "Johannesburg" on Google Maps to explore the city and find specific locations.

Maps.me: A popular offline maps app that allows you to download maps of Johannesburg for offline use.

TASTE OF THE SEASONS

While Johannesburg doesn't have extensive orchards or wineries within the city, it does offer a variety of markets and nearby farms. Here are three popular markets, farms, and wineries in and around Johannesburg:

Markets

Market on Main Location: Arts on Main, 264 Fox St, Johannesburg, 2094 Website: http://marketonmain.co.za/

Bryanston Organic & Natural Market Location: Culross Road (off Main Road), Bryanston, Johannesburg, 2191 Website: http://www.bryanstonorganicmarket.co.za/

Fourways Farmers Market Location: Montecasino Boulevard, Fourways, Johannesburg, 2191 Website: https://www.ffmarket.co.za/

Farms

Irene Dairy Farm Location: Nellmapius Drive, Irene, Pretoria, 0062 (near Johannesburg) Website: https://irenefarm.co.za/

Lindley Farmstead Location: 38 Leslie Rd, Glenferness, Johannesburg, 2191 Website: http://www.lindleyfarmstead.co.za/

Vaal Organic Farmers Market (held on Saturdays) Location: Stonehaven on Vaal, Sylviavale Ah, Vanderbijlpark, 1900 (south of Johannesburg) Website: https://stonehaven.co.za/

Orchards

Just Darling Farm and Venue Location: Plot 40, Farm Kliprivier 110, Kliprivier Road, Mulbarton, Johannesburg, South Africa Website: http://justdarling.co.za/

Random Harvest Indigenous Plant Nursery Location: Plot 57, Muldersdrift, Johannesburg, South Africa Website: https://www.randomharvest.co.za/

Walkerville Apple Orchards Location: Plot 78, Walkerville, Johannesburg, South Africa Website: Not available

Wineries

Walter Sisulu Botanical Gardens (offers wine tasting) Location: Malcolm Road, Poortvliet, Roodepoort, Johannesburg, South Africa Websitee: https://www.sanbi.org/gardens/walter-sisulu/

Nottinghill Wine Estate Location: Portion 2, Portion 8, Portion 11, Portion 14, N14, Muldersdrift, Johannesburg, South Africa Website: https://www.nottinghill.co.za/

Leriba Hotel and Spa (wine cellar and wine tastings available) Location: 245 End Ave, Clubview, Centurion, Johannesburg, South Africa Website: https://www.leriba.co.za/

Please note that the availability of these establishments may vary, and it's recommended to check their respective websites or contact them directly for the most up-to-date information on visiting hours, activities, and reservations.

READ OTHER BOOKS BY CZYK PUBLISHING

Eat Like a Local United States Cities & Towns

Eat Like a Local United States

Eat Like a Local- Oklahoma: Oklahoma Food Guide

Eat Like a Local- North Carolina: North Carolina Food Guide

Eat Like a Local- New York City: New York City Food Guide

Children's Book: Charlie the Cavalier Travels the World by Lisa Rusczyk

CZYKPublishing.com

Made in the USA
Columbia, SC
24 October 2024

44988951R00124